AT EASE WITH STRESS

'Riding the wind like a kite,
not just being buffeted by it'

AT EASE WITH STRESS

The approach of wholeness

WANDA NASH

Illustrated by David Parkins

Darton, Longman and Todd
London

First published in 1988 by
Darton, Longman and Todd Ltd
89 Lillie Road, London SW6 1UD

© 1988 Wanda Nash

Illustrations © 1988 Darton, Longman and Todd

ISBN 0 232 51777 0

British Library Cataloguing in Publication Data

Nash, Wanda
    All ease with stress : the approach of
wholeness.
    1. Man. Stress. Self-treatment
    I. Title
    158′.1

ISBN 0–232–51777–0

Phototypeset by Input Typesetting Ltd, London SW19 8DR
Printed and bound in Great Britain by Anchor Brendon Ltd,
Tiptree, Essex

This is essentially a do-it-yourself book.
Those areas of stress that need outside professional
help have not been addressed. While general suggestions
can improve general situations, it needs expert help to
treat stress that may have a pathological cause.

Contents

Introduction

Putting stress to work for you not against you.

Have you ever thought how much we *count* today?

- ☐ The number of pounds that we receive each week;
- ☐ the number of times we perform a task each month;
- ☐ the number of houses that are built . . .
- ☐ the number of patients that are seen . . .
- ☐ the number of votes that . . .
- ☐ the number of bombs . . .

these are things that *count*.

Then there is the importance today of being seen to be *accountable*.

- ☐ How many boxes have we ticked today?
- ☐ How many checklists have been completed?
- ☐ How many letters written?
- ☐ How many parts, items, results, totals . . .?

These are the things we have to *recount* – usually to someone in authority over us – about what we have been up to, in order to convince them we are valuable.

So what has happened to those things we can't count, or measure? Our inside hopes and terrors and dreams and hopes, our ideas and feelings and projections? Do they count?

Do you and I COUNT? For what does this book count? *It is about looking at the stress in our lives, how much it counts, and whether it counts for or against us.*

We all, without exception, experience stress, although we often try to deny it or eliminate it or send it underground.

This book is offered as a way of looking straight at it – where the stress comes from, what its roots are, how it has so much power over us – and then putting that power to work. DOING SOMETHING ABOUT IT. Just looking at it and recognizing it is the first 'doing' to do about it. There is so much energy within stress that usually the doing results in some change in our actions or our thought patterns or our feelings. This energy in stress can be destructive or constructive, and which way it goes often rests upon the way we *choose* to let it go, once we have realized what counts.

But first it means attending to things that cannot be counted. It means choosing to give some time to areas of ourselves that are personal and private and not for public consumption, and so are dis-counted. No one needs to know what we are up to, and the outward cost isn't significant, but the inward gain is without price.

People who look to a book about stress do so for different reasons. There are those who want an authoritative and crisp recipe to overcome hassles. There are those who want to deal with the stress of others. There are those who acknowledge the presence of stress only at times of crises, and there are those who want to turn to professional counselling and medical help. But this book is for ordinary people who know that self-help can often disarm crises, and who want to explore self-awareness from many different angles for themselves. It offers a variety of skills like a menu of ideas; it is up to readers to pick and choose among them what suits their particular taste. There are some signposts, too, which invite the reader to travel along a path and to discover where it leads them. It is a book whose intention is to prod and suggest, but it does not prescribe. That responsibility is left for each reader to take individually.

Almost without realizing it, each one of us can become more poised, more balanced, and more likely to turn into the person we want to be, by allowing space to each part which makes up the whole. Each part needs space to be aired and exercised in a conscious and balanced way, so the whole is neither distorted nor top-heavy. That sounds a rather preposterous claim, and there is a catch. This book does not offer one simple easy solution to the puzzles of life, it won't even take the puzzlement away. But as each part is recognized and given space, the sense of becoming fragmented and pulled apart by stress will lessen, and the sense of wholeness will increase and grow stronger. Gradually, being at ease among the inevitable stresses and strains of living will become a reality.

This book is primarily written with those in mind who want to use the stress they find in their lives to a strong end. The skills it describes can be useful to *anybody*. Although it will become clear that the author herself is a declared Christian, the tactics and techniques within these pages have enlivened the lives of many, whatever their declaration. It is about stress skills, and is certainly never intended to be an evangelising project; so perhaps those members of the Church who are looking for a more prominent input of scriptural terminology will be disappointed. To them it must be said, use it alongside your Bible, not in place of it!

How to use this book

The book can be used by individuals practising quietly and privately on their own; or some people may find working through it with a like-minded friend more helpful, trying out together which notions work and which don't. Others may feel it is useful to meet as a group, reading a chapter at a time and comparing notes about how it relates to their own lives and their own temperaments. Or some people may prefer discussing it with a one-to-one counsellor, exploring which bits are strengthening and which should be discarded. It can be looked upon as a map of the general territory of stress and its effects so that you can plot your own position. It may help to go through the various figures and charts, pin-pointing exactly where you are now and what applies to you and your own needs.

It may seem that there is an undue amount of 'I' and 'Me' in this text. This is a book about me coping with my stress, because that is a fairly important preliminary to helping others with theirs. The emphasis is not on self-absorption or self-importance, but most of the book tackles personal awareness in order then to go out and meet the problems of others. If I can recognize something of what is going on inside me, it is more likely that I will be empathetic towards what is happening inside someone else. There is only one person that I am actually in charge of and whose stress I can affect directly, and that is me. So until I can take that in hand, I shall probably only add to the stress of others.

One other suggestion. You may like to take an initial skim through the book. Then let it *mull*. After a while go back to the ideas that seemed to mean most to you, read them over and let them rumble away at a level just below your conscious thought. Don't waste energy trying to hang on to them – if they are going to be any good to you they will pop up again from time to time in your daily living, bringing a new shape with them each time they emerge. Like looking at something from different angles, so you get to see it as a whole. Whatever you like about this book has to be made your own: nothing can be imposed. It will need patience with yourself, but it will work. And gradually you will find yourself more at ease with stress.

In short:

The nub of the subject and content of the book lies in a short formula:

RECOGNIZE
RELATE
RELEASE
RELAX
REFLECT

These are the bones. Turn over to start putting them to work.

Part One

THE BASICS

1
Stress

What sort of image does the word 'stress' conjure up in your mind? It could be one of distress, or tense excitement, or of a spring being squeezed into a box with a tight-fitting lid. Is it a pressure cooker that is about to burst its safety valve? It may feel something like a tangle being pulled out in all directions, or a shrieking steam-engine bearing down the track that you can't get off. Perhaps your mind deals less

with images and more with reality, and you remember having to test and prove yourself in sport, or perform in public for the first time.

The word 'stress' nowadays means many different things to many different people. It is one of the words that has been overloaded lately with meanings which were not in its original use. Linguistically speaking, this was to describe the weight put upon various parts of speech – to 'stress a rhythm' or 'stress a point'. Today it has taken on the form of an umbrella term, under which anything goes when it describes a feeling of being pushed or squeezed, of being over-stretched or under-powered. It seems as though everyone can recognize something in their own lives which will immediately fit under the umbrella. And yet stress has still not been accurately defined to the satisfaction of all those who use it. This first part of the book will lay a foundation of how the word can be used for the everyday purposes of everyday people living with everyday stress in our everyday world. What to do about it will come later.

Other words which are frequently found in company with stress, are weight, tension, pressure, and strain. The connection between them in construction engineering is plain. Buildings are weighty and they have struts and beams to transfer that weight safely. Bridges bear pressure securely. Flyovers carry strain, and they have buttresses and pillars to conduct that strain into the ground. We live our lives among structures whose stress is so ordered that it actually increases their strength and function. The stress is directed and used.

Making order of the stress within us is one way of putting stress to work. Another is making use of stress that comes from without. Think how infuriating a shoelace is until it comes under tension, or how excruciating a violin sounds until its tension is exact. Then it sings. So applying stress appropriately can add excitement and richness.

Sometimes stress is essential to get us going:

Imagine a sleek new car parked outside your house.
It has been made to the highest standards of design, with

no expense spared. The engine is finely tuned, each part interacting with every other, smoothly and efficiently. The upholstery is enticing, the polished exterior superb. The tank is filled with the finest fuel, the day is fair and all is set to go. But, one thing is needed, without which the whole elaborate construction is useless, one vital spark: the tiny explosion which provides the pressure which compresses the piston to generate the power which will move the motor. In short, the pressure (stress) which gets the engine running and gets the car going.

Stress is about pressure and the reaction it produces. In human rather than engineering terms, it is the happenings around alarms and responses. That sounds simple enough, but over-simplification is deceiving. There are human alarms whenever there is challenge or change. Family decisions, examinations, interviews, pressure groups, elections, all work on a system of responses to alarms which use stress as a force to get things going.

But alarms can take on different characteristics, and also different people can respond to the same alarm differently. For instance:

☐ Alarms may be either disturbing or stimulating; they may produce panic or thrills. The same fair-ground ride will overwhelm some people with fear, and yet be thrilling for others.

☐ Alarms can be avoided or actively sought. Some people shy away from taking risks, while others get high on it.

☐ Alarms may come from deep within oneself, or they may come from outside. The fear of a disaster that is only imagined can be as great as the alarm of a real one.

Responses can be just as varied: they can be from an individual or a group; they can be conditioned or deliberate; they can be positive and constructive or negative and destructive; they may be appropriate or inappropriate.

Given that alarms and responses have a wide range and diversity, can a balance be gained within stress? How can we keep our peace of mind?

Peace of mind is not 'natural' to the majority of people living in Western civilization as we know it today. We hear our society commonly described as having lost its way; we are grasping at instant satisfactions to avoid gasping at a deeper emptiness. Peace of mind can be reached, but it has to be deliberately chosen, deliberately worked at, deliberately safeguarded. We all live somewhere in between peace and turbulence, usually hopping from one position to another like birds on a telegraph wire. Where along that line would *I* fit? Do I *want* to alter my point of balance?

Over-much stress or un-managed stress can bring a lot of trouble, but we can't do without it altogether. Stress is vitalizing, necessary, often enjoyable and constructive; if we look at it straight, we can learn to come to terms with both its effects and its management.

All in all, it makes it easier to unravel this entangled subject and its many ramifications if it is broken down into three parts:

☐ stressors – that is, those things which provoke alarms;
☐ stress-signs – that is, the effects which alarms produce; and
☐ stress-skills – the abundance of techniques which are at hand to make the most of stress, and lessen its harm. Most of these things we can develop for ourselves.

This last area, that of stress-*skills*, is the best bit: there are definite skills that can be purposefully learnt and applied which work for us, increasing or enjoyment and zest for living in spite of its risks and demands. Stress is an essential part of our lives and it would be dull and even dangerous to live without alarms. It is how we respond to the alarms that make us nice to know or not, and which determine whether we can be on good terms with our very selves.

2

Stressors

So 'stress' is what happens around alarms and the responses we make to them; it is made up of stressors, stress-signs, and stress-skills.

There is a great deal of discussion these days about our 'highly-stressed society'. In what ways is it different to previous periods of history? Men and women have lived through famine and disaster, plagues and poverty, jobless-ness, persecution and war before now, but there has never before been so much talk about 'high stress levels'. Why? What is it that holds extra alarm in the present day? It may be that there is a greater recognition of the far-reaching effects of stress; it may be that in the absence of a preoccu-pation such as a national war, our energies are insufficiently channeled outside ourselves; but probably more than either of these it has to do with deep and unmet issues that are philosophical and sociological.

Stress concerns the feeling of being pushed or squeezed or pulled or stretched. The pressures, weights, burdens that produce these reactions are called stressors, and they often come in the form of challenges to be met and decisions to be made. The effects they have are the subject of the next chapter, stress-signs; but here it is the nature of the stressors themselves which is being explored. It is not designed as a wallow in gloom and doom, but to help indentify and recog-nize what is going on around us. Until we can be clear about the situation in which we are living, it is difficult to be clear about how we can act constructively. It's not until I am aware that my windscreen is spattered with mud and splattered with insects that I actually take the necessary action to clean it – and suddenly I wonder why I didn't do it before.

Stressors can be approached at three levels: firstly, there are those that are immediate – they come from outside ourselves and are objective; secondly, there are the cultural currents which underlie the more obvious layer; and thirdly, there are those that stem from our individual temperaments. The following description is based on these three levels.

LEVEL A:
COMMON IMMEDIATE STRESSORS*

☐ TRANSITIONS – things that involve a change of direction; this can include major life events such as birth, marriage, death, and also passing upheavals like moving house, changing jobs, examinations, interviews, illness, loss, theft, court cases, accidents, separation, even holidays.

☐ RELATIONSHIPS – things that involve on-going interaction with others, such as the family, employment, tiresome neighbours, landlord harassment, marital difficulty, elderly relatives at home.

☐ ENVIRONMENT – things that belong to the external situation in which we live, such as poor housing, overcrowding, rich neighbourhood, noise, pollution, traffic, street violence, advertising pressures, unemployment, competition, sport, pressure at work, too little money, powerlessness, too much power, social culture ('keeping up with the Jones'), demands by peers, nuclear threat, AIDS threat, etc, etc.

☐ HASSLES – things that constitute lesser annoyances:

* Physical pain and disability are a consideration of their own. Different aspects of pain or disability could fit into any of the following six categories; pain, illness, chronic disease, and even some disability can be the result of stress or the cause of stress. Everything in this book can apply in the presence or absence of illness and pain, and it would need to be double the size if every aspect were to be pursued and specified!

petty tangles, temporary upsets, domestic trials, imagined difficulties.

☐ ACQUIRED SYMBOLS of stress, which can lead to obsessional phobias, such as fear of mice, dogs, spiders, undergrounds, heights, lifts, crowds, open spaces: anything that becomes a symbol of anxiety or a focus of a conviction of loss of control.

☐ MEANINGLESSNESS – a profound absenting of things that give value to life, resulting in feelings of rejection, withdrawal of purpose, lack of direction or goal. This may be the result of external circumstances such as bereavement, redundancy, divorce, excommunication, or may be an internal loss of faith and trust which overlaps the next level of stressors.

External and objective stressors such as those in Level A have always been around. Whether they trigger behaviour that is constructive or destructive depends more upon *how we respond* to them, than upon what they are. However, the reponses we make may be aggravated by the next level of stressor, and it is here that the historic differences are important.

They are characterized by three very basic losses:

1. the loss of the traditional sense of 'place' in society,
2. the loss of widely accepted and stable moral signposts, and
3. the loss of obvious role models.

So today it is easy to feel we are each as it were on our own, without a familiar map, having had many of our heroes and heroines levelled, and their weaknesses exposed. This means that more or less anything goes, any doors may be opened and any new paths followed.

The following are some of the deep currents that are new to our age:

LEVEL B:
COMMON UNDERCURRENT STRESSORS

There is:
- [ ] an increased feeling of *anonymity*: the individual is felt to be a cog in the wheel, a number, a unit without worth.
- [ ] an increased *competitiveness*: people are climbing over each other's backs; there is a feeling that you're no good if you're not winning, and a terror among many of being left behind.
- [ ] an increased *artificiality*: more is synthetic, more is processed, more is chemically manipulated, including food, textiles, horticulture, building construction, genetics, etc. The individual has little control over what is available to use.
- [ ] more is *disposable*: there is a transience, instability, restlessness around, and even relationships are affected; they are sometimes felt to be not worth mending.
- [ ] an increased *spacelessness*: houses are crowded together, many shops and offices are windowless, transport is crammed both inside and out.
- [ ] more *passivity*: there is a complicated network of medical, legal, and social constrictions which tend to reduce men and women into passive receivers – they are 'done to' Any sort of active response is discouraged (e.g. in a traffic jam, in a queue, in response to complaints), and physical exertion is less common (fewer bread-winners today have to hunt or sweat for their product). Aggravation and tension are built up but releasing it is increasingly impracticable, particularly at work.
- [ ] increased *stimulation*: as well as this reduced activity, we have to put up with a daily, even hourly intrusion into our lives of a calculated inflation of our appetites for food, alcohol, sex, acquisition, self-indulgence, vengeance, hatred and horror. Images of violence and depravity are no longer kept out of our homes or away from our children. Is this type of titillation counter-balanced by an

equally powerful stimulation of interest in values that are positive?

☐ increased *speed* of ideas, and instructions which are soon replaced by others: in the media, advertisements and competitions face us with constant choices and decisions – shall I buy? Shall I resist or respond? Shall I stay where I am or move across?

☐ a new high value put on *change*: not only on to 'improved' models in technology but also in organizations, ideas, policies. Little weight is given to tradition, but change is valued for the sake of novelty. This is most obvious in fashion, personal decoration, domestic equipment and consumer ware, and is hyped-up by advertising. The speed (as above) and diversity of change, have together earned the title for our age as one of OVERCHOICE, resulting in distraction and confusion.

☐ more *questioning* that is radical, disturbing, insatiable, both in public matters and private philosophy. Many people live in a quagmire of uncertainty. A student recently described this state as travelling on 'a spaghetti-junction of doubt'. The unthinkable is now becoming thinkable, expanding vast areas of insecurity.

☐ a spread of *confusion of direction*: this has contributed to and results from several of the above undercurrents. The flexibility of those moral frameworks that do exist has had a double effect – on the one hand they are insufficient as safety-nets for the majority of people, and on the other there is an increase of sub-cultures which provide boundaries that are rigid. These are felt to be secure, but they are also separatist and intolerant.

☐ in some cases an *exaggerated allegiance* to a cause, or meaning, has resulted: for instance fringe sects which confine young people within restrictive dogmas, nationalism that runs riot as terrorism, occult practices and extremisms.

☐ and, lastly, but perhaps most pervasive, an underlying stressor that is 'new' to our times is the *constant hyper-arousal* of our senses as a distraction from looking at emptiness. Sounds, loud music, pictures, colours, move-ment, words, invade our personal space continuously unless we take conscious steps to avoid them. It seems as though a lack of external stimulation is something to be dreaded rather than being seen as a chance to mull and to muse.

All these pressures add up to the most stressful questions of all:

> Who am I?
> Where am I going?
> Am I loved or lovable?

It would be easy – and perhaps more comfortable – to sit back and lay the whole blame for today's high stress levels on the above cultural currents and the objective stressors which they aggravate. But that would be to accept that we are powerless robots, responding as programmed to each situation. In fact, we are proud to be individual, and to react individually.

Each one of us has a different temperament and a different capacity for 'taking' stress: it is not the alarms themselves but the manner in which we respond to those alarms that produces the turbulence within us. How much we allow things to happen around us, and how much we decide to take charge of our own responses is crucial. So the third level of stressor is about such internal factors as:

LEVEL C

☐ our own physical make-up
☐ our conditioning
☐ our capacity for stress
☐ our expectation of ourselves
☐ the expectation of others towards ourselves
☐ the projections of others upon us
☐ the hold that our imaginations have upon us.

Arguably, the greatest stressor of all is that which I put on myself – the targets and standards I set for myself – which involve my sense of self-respect, my sense of competence or inadequacy, my high or low ambition, the way in which I use my imagination, and the degree to which I hold myself responsible for my own behaviour. Once again there are two extremes.

If I expect too little of myself, I can see myself as a victim of circumstances. My view of myself is epitomized by such phrases as:

'I couldn't manage that.'
'Nobody understands, nobody cares.'
'I can't cope . . .'
'If only . . .'

and a common feeling that is in all of us at some time or other – 'Poor little me!' – when fear, anxiety, and the conviction that I am hard done by, seems to be overwhelming.

On the other hand, I can expect too much of myself. I

can become dependent on my own sense of control over myself. I can become hooked on that marvellous feeling that I can cope with anything. I can become euphoric that I get through so much work, I need so little sleep, so little to eat, can survive so much pressure. When I continue to feed off my own adrenalin and to prove to myself how much control I have, it becomes a self-perpetuating spiral. Until it collapses.

The same stressor that makes one person feel powerfully in control may be fraught with challenge and despair for another. The feeling that the threat is controllable is thrilling to some, while to others the merest risk that the threat may *not* be controllable reduces their coping powers to jelly. The difference in the way people handle similar situations depends partly upon the personality type they were born with, and partly upon their own assessment and awareness of their abilities – or at least how they have got used to seeing those abilities. The control we have over alarms coming at us may be limited, but there is more room for us to control how we react to them.

This has been a somewhat heavy chapter, but it has a brighter conclusion. In the face of all the alarms and uncertainties listed earlier, it is hardly surprising that there is such an increase in self-doubt and self-analysis today. There is a great advantage – if I understand and take account of the various conditions which surround me, I myself can set the goals that I know suit me and which I want to reach. In addition, I can choose – to a certain extent – what I want to carry with me, rather than having to submit to the luggage which social convention wants to put upon me; or at least I can be responsible for shifting it around and changing the way in which it is packed, and decide for myself what I want to throw out. In the process I am likely to achieve a more satisfying degree of maturity and equilibrium. Perhaps I may learn too that life cannot be lived wholly without risk, but risk can add zest to life. And that is what Part Two is all about.

3

Stress-signs

The previous pages described in some detail those things which hold alarm for us. Whatever the alarm, we all carry within us a basic package of physiological responses which developed along with our humanness as soon as we evolved as hunters. In the primeval state, when we were presented with an alarm, there was one basic decision which had to be made, and our survival depended upon it. The decision had to be instantaneous: when a dinosaur came bearing down upon the cave man there was little chance for him to experiment with alternative options. In a split second he had to decide – fight or flight? – no hanging about weighing pros and cons. To help him in this decision, every system in his body automatically went on to red alert, without any conscious command on his part. Each system in his body adapted itself to make every possible ounce of energy available to him, and every sense picked up messages from the situation to inform his decision.

We are seldom challenged by dinosaurs these days, but we still have the basic response pattern as a blue-print in our genes. It is now overlaid and sometimes short-circuited, but the basic bodily reaction is still with us. In fact, it is fundamental to both our nervous system and to our muscular functioning.

The chart in Figure 1 (pages 28 and 29) is an outline of (A) the basic package, (B) what usually happens next, and (C) what can happen if the tension accumulates because it is not practical to react by either fighting or running, and we can't 'let off steam' physically.

Our initial responses are necessary, vital and energizing;

they are outlined in column A. The effects they produce, listed in column B, are appropriate, and our survival often depends on them; they provide us with coping powers, excitement and exhilaration. Every race, sex and culture of humankind reacts with these basic patterns. The difference between us comes after column B.

The success of this simple pattern of alarm and response is proved by the very fact we are still here, but the difficulties we experience today are due to various factors which have compounded it. These are:

☐ The alarms we now meet are more frequent, more numerous, and more varied.

☐ Our temperaments are more complex and our responses range from those that are delicate, to the toughest.

☐ Our behaviour is no longer limited to simple survival but has to adapt continually to get on with a lot of other people.

☐ Due to the heavy demands made on it, our nervous system has learnt to short-cut some of the responses, so that they are triggered in inappropriate ways; they can then become habits that are difficult to break.

☐ There are now too many obstacles in the way for carrying through the whole sequence of alarm > responses > discharge of energy. Think how often follow-through action is thwarted: in queues and waiting-rooms, at work, in traffic jams, through aborted plans, frustrated desires, blind starts. In all such instances tension is hoarded.

When energy is *habitually* locked in, then and only then do the effects in columns C and D become real. It is useful to be aware of these possibilities, but Parts Two and Three will deal with practical ways of stopping such a downhill course. Energy that has been stock-piled can be diverted into skills which enlarge our lives and enrich our experience. So don't be discouraged by the chart – the process is not irreversible.

There is another level of our response to stress which perhaps affects the people around us even more than our

Figure 1. **Positive effects of instant alarm**

A. BASIC PACKAGE OF
RESPONSE TO ALARM

B. PHYSIOLOGICAL
FUNCTION

Instantaneous rush of hormone adrenalin into bloodstream	– to raise total physical and mental alertness in order to deal with challenge. 'Survival' emotions are aroused: fear/self-doubt or anger/ aggression
Liver is stimulated to release the energy in the body that is stored as fat and sugar	– to provide maximum energy for instant use.
Raised rate of breathing	– to increase supply of oxygen in the blood.
Raised pulse rate	– to increase speed of transport of oxygen to every muscle where energy will be used.
Muscle tone is tensed	inhibited readiness for action.
Mind alerted	– all mental faculties focused on decision-making.
All senses aroused	– to receive messages interpreting the situation. Sight, hearing, taste, smell all sharpened. In some, touch also becomes more acute.
Digestive process inhibited	– to divert energy for priority use in limbs.
Perspiration increases	– to cool body down in the event of extra exercise.
Need to empty bladder, and perhaps bowels	– to lessen body weight.
Hair follicles tighten causing 'goose pimples', tingling skin	– to raise hair as an aspect of threat (especially in animals).
Heightened emotional tension	– to motivate extreme effort.

At this stage, coping abilities have been alerted, danger can be met appropriately, and all is well. It is only if energy is *not* discharged, redirected, or defused, that the process continues into the next stages – C and D.

C. RESULTING DISCOMFORT IF ENERGY IS INSUFFICIENTLY DISCHARGED

D. LONG-TERM EFFECTS IF TENSION BECOMES HABITUAL

C. RESULTING DISCOMFORT IF ENERGY IS INSUFFICIENTLY DISCHARGED	D. LONG-TERM EFFECTS IF TENSION BECOMES HABITUAL
Person is left 'on edge', 'pent up'; tendency to worry is increased; high frustration.	Impatience, over-exacting of self and others; difficulty with sleeping > insomnia; development of anxiety habits.
Difficulty in calming down, cannot relax; may become hyper-active.	Irritability, tiredness, exhaustion; build up of cholesterol (large fat globules) in tiny coronary vessels.
Deep sighing, breathlessness.	May develop into hyperventilation, fainting, dizziness.
Racing pulse; raised blood pressure; flushed face.	Palpitations; headache; extreme demands on heart can predispose to heart disease.
Tension remains in muscles, which register pain from spasm and exhaustion.	Aching body, especially back, neck, shoulders, hips; limbs may shake involuntarily.
Impulsive behaviour; irrational decisions.	Hyper-arousal; imbalanced thinking; powers of concentration will become exhausted and attention and memory be affected; increase of anxiety.
Dilated pupils tire eyes; edginess experienced at loud noises, bright lights; tolerance levels lowered; pain level lowered.	Headache; withdrawal from ordinary social activity.
Dry mouth; loss of appetite; nausea ('butterflies' in stomach).	Halitosis; indigestion; pre-conditions for the formation of gastric ulcers; sluggish bowel may cause constipation, piles.
Clammy hands and feet; sweaty body.	Nervous rashes; soreness in crevices; eczema, spots, acne.
Frequency of urination, elimination.	Stress incontinence; irritable bowel syndrome, diverticulitis.
Hair loss.	Baldness not conspicuously affected!
Crying, shouting; mood-swings, 'moodiness', irrational behaviour; nervous laughter; show of over-confidence; testing the limits; petty crime; aggressive behaviour.	May turn to either extreme: euphoria to mask anxiety or withdrawal to hide from anxiety. Expression of anger, rage as release from tension, frustration; onset of depression; resort to violence.

physical reactions, and that is our moods. Moods and emotions are coloured by our hormones and genetic make-up, which is why different people feel so differently about the same situations. They also reflect the conditioning we received as children, the attitudes we have developed through our social education, and the living conditions in which we find ourselves. Having said all that, there still remains a large area where we can take the responsibility for the consequences of our moods, and the behaviour that follows on from them.

Managing our emotions is a theme that will be returned to many times. This is the point at which the stress-signs that are emotional should be outlined. The principle is the same: where tension has been built up, unable to be resolved or discharged, there will be signposts of stress. Perhaps 'self-control' has been so emphasized that the underlying stress is denied, but where these signs persist, it is important to consider taking stress-skills seriously.

Figure 2 charts the usual course of emotional response. The same responses can be the result of too many demands (overwork, large family, many commitments) or too few demands (being without work, loneliness, rejection). Too much social activity can produce similar stress-signs as boredom, disappointment, jealousy. Either ends of the scale may display irritability, irrational mood swings, nervous habits, the use of addictive substances as props, a show of over-confidence by talking and laughing too loudly, or a show of lack of confidence by withdrawal and apparent sullenness. Fussiness and indecision, not wanting to commit oneself, and compensatory behaviour are all signs of stress.

If these things are recognized for what they are, they can be counteracted. Stress is like an electrical charge and I have to decide whether I am going to adapt to it or whether I am going to be blown. I can fix a 3, 5 or 13 amp fuse and thereby put myself in control of that charge, or I can just let it happen and risk a breakdown. Figure 2 demonstrates the progress of emotional stress, and where conscious stress skills can divert it.

Figure 2. **The course of emotional response**

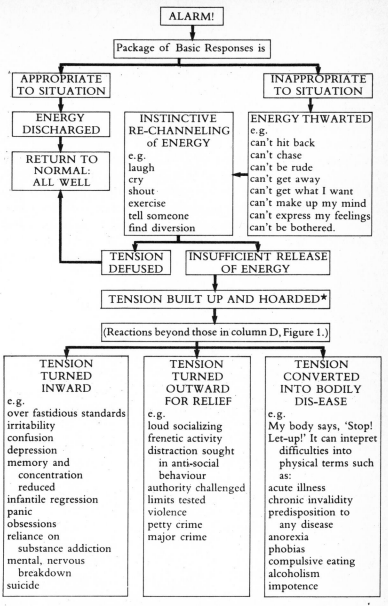

```
                        ┌──────────┐
                        │ ALARM!   │
                        └────┬─────┘
                             ▼
              ┌──────────────────────────────┐
              │ Package of Basic Responses is │
              └──────────────────────────────┘
```

APPROPRIATE TO SITUATION		INAPPROPRIATE TO SITUATION

ENERGY DISCHARGED	INSTINCTIVE RE-CHANNELING of ENERGY	ENERGY THWARTED
RETURN TO NORMAL: ALL WELL	e.g. laugh cry shout exercise tell someone find diversion	e.g. can't hit back can't chase can't be rude can't get away can't get what I want can't make up my mind can't express my feelings can't be bothered.

TENSION DEFUSED	INSUFFICIENT RELEASE OF ENERGY

TENSION BUILT UP AND HOARDED★

(Reactions beyond those in column D, Figure 1.)

TENSION TURNED INWARD	TENSION TURNED OUTWARD FOR RELIEF	TENSION CONVERTED INTO BODILY DIS-EASE
e.g. over fastidious standards irritability confusion depression memory and concentration reduced infantile regression panic obsessions reliance on substance addiction mental, nervous breakdown suicide	e.g. loud socializing frenetic activity distraction sought in anti-social behaviour authority challenged limits tested violence petty crime major crime	e.g. My body says, 'Stop! Let-up!' It can intepret difficulties into physical terms such as: acute illness chronic invalidity predisposition to any disease anorexia phobias compulsive eating alcoholism impotence

★ unless Stress–skills are successfully applied. It is at this point that the skills described in this book come into use.

If the hoarding of stress and its effects on our behaviour are not intercepted, then the news is bad. However, the main part of this book is good news: that there *are* ways and skills and attitudes that can be deliberately developed to channel, redirect or defuse that built-up tension. It's a question of avoiding the harmful effects of stress, and harnessing its motivating and energizing effects. It all begins with acknowledging and recognizing the cause and effects, the stressors and stress-signs, not only in others but deep within ourselves. The bad news may be painful and the signs of it are hurtful; many people go to great lengths to distract themselves from looking at it and to convince themselves the danger isn't there. But for those who do look hard and decide to improve their coping skills, the rewards are great. You'll know yourself better, get on with life better, and others will like being with you.

This whole chapter can be summed up in a simple formula –

If stress attacks   EASE
there are risks of   DISEASE;
until skills produce RELEASE.

4
Stress-skills

'Skill' is a very ancient word. In the early languages which contributed to English it was an important word, meaning to distinguish, discern, differentiate, decide, give a reason for, combining knowledge and ability in practice. It is just these qualities that lie behind all the methods and techniques and attitudes which put stress to work for us, and not against us. These are ways of making sure that stressors and stress-signs do not take charge of life, but instead put charge into it. We all know the feeling of being heavy and uselessly dispirited, but Dame Julian, as long ago as the fourteenth century, said that approaching life with 'heaviness and vain sorrow' could be 'un-skillful'. Just to know that there *are* skills that change heaviness into something more positive is a start!

First of all, there are the instinctive ways we cope with feelings of tension – laughing, joking, crying; taking a break; talking it out; finding a distraction in sport, entertainment, excercise, and so on. But, when these instinctive ways of behaving don't seem enough, further stress-skills come into play.

There is an abundance of stress-skills to be discovered, nourished, and put to use. Not all of them suit everybody, and each person can scan the possibilities and decide what works best for them.

Underlying all the stress-skills is the one common factor of *discernment* – the ability to recognize and acknowledge particular strands in a situation. Many situations of stress feel like a tangled knot of coloured threads – the more you pull at it the worse it gets. But if the different strands can be gradually disentangled, the situation becomes easier. It depends as much on the recognition and discernment of each strand as the ability to follow it through.

It is easier to grasp the range of stress-skills if they are loosely grouped:

1. First and foremost is the *recognition of the power and pressure of stressors* quite independently of whether I am 'good' or 'bad', 'clever' or 'dull'. It often takes considerable courage to admit – even to myself – that stress is affecting me, because our society has become inflated with the merits of keeping cool. It's as though the recognition of stress was in itself deflating to a person's image, whereas in truth it is both strong and wise to know and understand the tensions that have to be dealt with.

> Sometimes it seems easier to boast about how much I am coping with, than to come to grips with what it is costing. It's more ego-boosting to get the admiring response 'I don't know how you manage it,' than to face how much it is taking out of me. The actual recognition of difficulties is the first step in reducing stress; getting hooked on other people's admiring responses can increase stress.

2. There are skills to be used in *identifying and acknowledging the stress-signs* that have been listed in Figure 1, column A, as they happen. They are all observable in one's self, and most of them are observable in others. Having become familiar with them, it is a useful practice to go through the list, working out which stress-signs can be brought under conscious control, and which are affected only indirectly by conscious effort.

> I can't for instance, do much about my goose pimples, but I can learn to control the rate of my breathing and modify my breathlessness. I can't do a lot about my digestive system closing down, but I can learn to relax my abdominal muscles in such a way that the continual tightness around my digestive organs loosens.

3. There are the skills used in *getting to know our own capacity*

for stress, and becoming familiar with the set of tools we each have for coping with it.

> Am I a mini, a tractor, a limousine or a racer?
> What is the speed at which I am most comfortable?
> Can I recognize the sound of my own engine, the continual hum of patter inside me?
> Is my tool-kit rusty from lack of care, or dusty from lack of use, or obsolete and needing replacement?
> What am I best at? What are my weak points?

4. There are skills attached to *allowing ourselves to have strong feelings*. Even knowing they are there isn't always enough; sometimes they need to be given permission to be let out and expressed openly. Owning strong feelings and channelling them with the least harm needs specific skills; among them is using assertion properly and accepting the consequences of the way I speak and act.

When I feel angry or depressed or resentful or vindictive,

35

there is a limit to how much I can hold in. If it remains in the dark for too long it will fester. It would be better to admit it, at least to myself, and take deliberate steps to get it out of my system – without hurt to others. Similarly, sometimes I feel happy or hopeful or ebullient when those close to me are not, and I have to find ways of expressing my feelings without demanding too much from them. I may need to learn how to use my imagination, freeing it on things that are positive, but controlling it when it feeds my fear.

5. The skills of *meditation* add depth to all the forms of self-awareness mentioned so far. Different methods of meditation emphasize the technique of gaining control over bodily stress-signs, or of getting in touch with inner resources of strength, equilibrium, reassurance, and a reliance upon the power of God.

Recognizing my own make-up is one of the basics of meditation. Making friends with what I find is another. Many people discover a closer walk with things of the spirit which puts everything else into place.

6. Perhaps the most important thing of all, the skill of *finding and keeping meaning and direction* in my way of life and whatever gives it purpose, and finding and keeping the support that sustains it. It has been said that meaninglessness is the greatest stressor of all, and that much of our search for 'having a good time' is in order to avoid it.

If I am uneasy with the direction of my life, I have a choice; either to alter it in spite of the inconvenience and uncertainty, or to carry on and fill its emptiness with distractions. If the activity is sufficiently frenetic, and the noise is loud enough and the lights glittering enough, this tactic may work for a time. But it won't begin to equate with the assurance gained from holding real meaning which goes on growing throughout life.

7. Then there are skills of *objectifying and externalizing*. Many of these are learnt techniques which help to sort out issues that have become entangled in subjective emotions: worry, anxiety and hassle.

> I want to know how to stand back and sort out the
> different coloured strands which go into a tangle. I need
> to be able to decide which ones I am responsible for and
> can unknot, and which ones I have to lay on one side.

8. There are many skills that apply to *relationships*. Often
the negative stress within a relationship can be defused by
attentive listening.

> Do I hear what is NOT said as clearly as I hear what IS
> said? Can I presume to understand totally what the
> other person is feeling? It was a Red Indian chief who
> said, 'Don't know how other fella feel unless have
> walked two mile in other fella moccasin.'

9. There is a large group of *organizational* skills which help
to alleviate and manage stress. To some degree or other
everybody has experience of these, because they are part of
our growing-up. However they can all be improved, and
the more efficient they become the better our use of stress
will be. These essential practical skills are used whenever I

☐ decide between this priority or that;
☐ make a list of my commitments and rank them in order
  of urgency;
☐ plan the goals I want to attempt, and adjust them so that
  they are realistic and not wildly unobtainable;
☐ manage the time I have in order to make full use of it;
☐ organize my tasks and pace myself to meet them;
☐ co-operate with other people and, instead of feeling I have
  to do it all myself, let them in on it and share the work
  and the responsibility – and the rewards.

10. Last, but by no means least, there are all the skills
necessary for *looking after the body*. It is fundamental that we
keep our bodies in good health if we want to make the most
of the effects of stress. A body that is fit can stand up to and
enjoy an extraordinary degree of stress. On the other hand,
it is well accepted medically that over-stress is a condition
that lowers resistance to many stressors and heightens the

ill-effects of stress-signs. This situation has a spin-off that spirals downwards; for instance:

- ☐ If I get worn out with coping, I won't be bothered with cooking. If I don't eat a balanced meal I will feel more worn out. So it is important to eat proper food.
- ☐ If my muscles are continually tense from stress they will ache, so I won't exercise them. If I don't exercise them it is difficult to get rid of the tenseness. So it is important to have regular exercise.
- ☐ If I become over-tired I will be more likely to worry and feel inadequate. So I will try harder and become more over-tired. So it is important to sleep enough.
- ☐ If I continue to be worn out, tense and over-tired, I am more likely to get minor illnesses and to have accidents. If this state becomes habitual, I am more likely to be overtaken by major diseases. Therefore it is totally essential to make sure I eat, drink, sleep and exercise in a way that is responsible.

In addition to learning how to read the signs of my body myself, modern technology can be used to help us detect stress levels. Some people use biofeedback machines, for instance, which monitor the stressful activity within the body and help reinforce relaxation methods. Computerized exercise cycles can be useful monitors also, and cassette recorders have a valuable role to play.

Relaxation is one of the skills which are necessary in looking after the body. The differences between ordinary relaxation, a diversion that is resting, and deep releasing relaxation will be described later. Different techniques have been developed over the centuries, and the skill of breath control is part of some of these. Whatever method is chosen, many people find that they can tackle all the objective skills – as well as some of the subjective ones – in a clearer, freer way after they have relaxed. Some 'experts' hold that deep relaxation is the most important skill of all, but the aim of this book is to leave it up to each reader to choose which skills are most relevant to each individual.

The following pages will expand all the stress-skills touched upon here. Now the basic foundation of stressors, stress-signs and stress-skills has been laid, each reader can build upon it their own personal framework. The supports they choose will help them to enjoy the thrust and zest that stress brings to their lives, without collapsing under its strain.

——CHRISTIAN OUTLOOK——

The whole of this discussion, seen from the point of view of some Christian traditionalists, could be said to concern the tendentious area of 'shoulds' and 'oughts' and 'musts' and 'don'ts':

> You *MUST* . . .
> I *OUGHT* . . .
> He *SHOULD* . . .
> . . . No *DON'T*

This looks like the language of morals, so 'stressed' behaviour gets mixed up with 'sinful' behaviour.

It is at this point that multitudes of people switch off from Christianity. It seems as though stressed behaviour is indeed seen as sinful behaviour and then the situation is compounded by guilt. In the minds of many people, received Christianity says that feeling irritable, angry, blaming, self-careful, indulgent, demanding, or depressed is evidence of sin: Christ – our perfect example – was none of these, so we shouldn't be either. Wasn't he? Did Christ never feel stress?

> Christ was irritated by his disciples,
>   when they continued to be obstinate, and by the
>   non-fruiting fig tree on the way to his trial.
> He was angry with the temple money lenders,
>   when he whipped them from their stalls.
> He was acrimonious to the Pharisees,
>   when they pressed him with questions cleverly
>   calculated to catch him out.

He sometimes put his own needs first,
    sleeping when his friends were in acute fear,
    over-riding the claims of his mother.
He enjoyed feasts and wine; he wasn't a kill-joy,
    he brought abundance of living.
He was tough on his followers,
    demanding they left their homes and travelled
        without carrying food or money or extra clothes.

Did Christ live a bland, protected, non-stressed life? As a human he knew about stressors and he knew the skills to deal with them. He knew that too much stress produced stressed behaviour. He didn't judge stressed behaviour as sin. So where have we got it wrong?

Jesus Christ, as a created human being, acknowledged God the Father as greater and (for us) more unknowable than anything we can conceive; that God is immeasurable immensity.
He didn't compress God into the image of his own super-ego. We do!

He superseded all the intricate laws of good behaviour that were insisted upon by his own culture with the one guideline, 'Love the Lord with all your heart and strength and soul and mind, and your neighbour as yourself.'
He didn't surround himself with oughts and shoulds and musts in order to earn God's attention and approval. We do!

He dealt with the unease he found within him directly; if he was thirsty he said so, without implying it was the other person's fault for not providing drink. If he was tired, or needed quiet, or was rough-handled by the authorities he dealt with it directly, without putting the blame for its cause on to other people.
He didn't project the things he found uncomfortable within him on to others and blame them for them, thus protecting his own self-righteousness. We do!

Our tendency as human beings is to project the dark things

inside us that we don't wish to see on to other people; we don't like the look of our needs, perhaps because they mean we are less in control than we pretend to be, so we make out they aren't there. It's so much easier to say it's your fault that I feel angry, tired, depressed, disillusioned: then I can remain unblemished because the blame lies outside me.

In turn, that means that I can hang on to a very high (and complimentary) expectation of myself, and I will put myself under more strain in order to live up to these high ideas. When I don't manage to reach the standards I have set for myself I feel guilty, and fear I may not be lovable or capable or approved. I can't bear that, so again it has to be someone else's fault and the vicious circle winds me tighter and tenser and I become even more intolerant.

If we pause to look at our feelings of stress objectively, we will discover they are
> part of our genetic *make-up*,
> before being part of our *morality*.

Then we could so lessen the burden of guilt, that we could do something about the stress. Jesus was aware of his own needs, and he didn't twist and turn and contrive to disguise them and pretend they weren't there. But nor did he allow the stressed behaviour to become habitual and lead to separation from God. That's where the nature of sin is to be found, in separation and distancing from God.

This fundamental difference will be expanded as the book progresses, and will touch on our projections of bad and inflated feelings on to others and on to God. These things are at the bottom of much of our stress. It is a profound misunderstanding to equate stressed behaviour with sinful behaviour; it is not so much a question of switching off from this as of latching on to our greatest hope. God is with us, Emmanuel, alongside us, Maranatha; he knows our stress full well and has provided the means to cope with it.

The Celts had a very pragmatic, affirmative faith. They knew that God was with them everywhere, accompanying and empowering them. As they went about their daily chores they would chant:

> I am walking with the Father,
> I am walking with the Son,
> I am walking with the Spirit –
>   the Three-fold All-kindly –
> Ho! Ho! Ho! Three in One!

How could they fail in such company?

Summary of Part One:
Categories of Today's Stressors

and the SKILLS which can be developed to deal with them.

Relationships
Appropriate SKILLS include how to:
- [ ] listen;
- [ ] manage my own strong emotions – expressing love and joy creatively, recognizing anger and blame as usually inefficient, and that sorrow can be a growing-point;
- [ ] use touch;
- [ ] find time.

Hassles
Appropriate skills include how to:
- [ ] disentangle the strands that have made up the knot;
- [ ] deal with each separately;
- [ ] keep cool and objective;
- [ ] see the other point of view and try to find a gate through the fence (anybody can find offence – it's the clever ones who find a gate!).

Meaninglessness
Appropriate skills include how to:
- [ ] find out my own values –
  interest in others?
  purpose in life?
  direction of life?
  stimulation?
  family?
  money?
  possessions and power?
  social life?
  impressing others with Me?
  discovering God and his purpose?;
- [ ] find or set-up a like-minded support group.

Transitions
Appropriate skills include how to:
- [ ] recognize unusual level of high stress;
- [ ] prepare and practise coping tactics;
- [ ] take special care to keep body fit, and mind, spirit, emotions filled;
- [ ] plan time, actions, tasks, etc. – make lists, delegate responsibilities, design realistic goals;
- [ ] be pleased with achievement!

Environment
Appropriate skills include how to:
- [ ] decide what cannot be changed and adapt to it;
- [ ] work towards changing what can and should be changed;
- [ ] be careful and wise, distinguishing between the two.

Acquired Symbols
Where such things as crowds, open spaces, water, spiders, dogs or germs become such stressors that ordinary living becomes difficult, professional help should be sought.

Part Two

STRESS-SKILLS FOR WHOLENESS

5
Wholeness

This is the nub of the matter – wholeness.

The idea of being a complete shape is crucial. Wholeness does not mean that we all have to be complete spheres, or that we all have to be perfect, nor does it mean that having reached a certain shape we stay there, static. An amoeba and a bean-bag are whole; they are perfectly adjusted to the functions for which they exist and they both adapt perfectly to the demands made upon them, but they are both constantly changing shape. Yet what they are, their identity, remains unchanged; they keep their wholeness.

The amoeba's wholeness is different to the bean-bag's; they can't be compared. So each person's wholeness is unique to themselves, and cannot be compared with another's. Only that person can know what their particular completeness is for themselves, no one else can tell them.

If stress is seen as part of the process of becoming whole, then from that angle it is 'good for you'. When stress is recognized, the energy locked up within it can be put to work to fill out our wholeness. Some people speak as though all stress should be banished, and all signs of stress done away with; certainly harmful effects have to be met and dealt with, but there is so much drive and growth within stress that without it we should be deprived of deep sources of energy which can positively help towards wholeness.

Some languages use one and the same word for *crisis* and *opportunity*. It would help many of us to think of them in the same way.

STRESS IS *PART OF* WHOLENESS,
NOT *APART FROM* IT.

This chapter will address three questions:
- ☐ What is wholeness?
- ☐ What *use* is the idea of wholeness?
- ☐ How do I recognize my own wholeness?

WHAT IS WHOLENESS?

The word 'whole' comes from an ancient stem which, like the word 'skill', was common in many of the early European languages. It shares its historic origin with several related words, all of which are important. It is of enormous significance that the one common root has produced:

> Hail! – for welcome, social contact.
> Hale – robustness, for action.
> Health – soundness of body, mind, and spirit.
> Holy – for being hallowed, blessed.
> Holiday – for rest and play.
> WHOLE
> Taken together, these words describe our wholeness.

A useful symbol of wholeness is in Figure 3. This model has four parts. The classical description of a person's make-up is of heart, soul, and strength – that is, feelings, spirit and body; this lacks the fourth part, that of the 'mind'. It's not always realized that it is Christ who is recorded as adding this fourth part, mind, to the usual list that makes up a person's complete commitment.

This model marks the 'mind' for *thinking*, the 'body' for *doing*, the 'soma' for *feeling* (that is, both emotional and sensory feeling) and the 'spirit' for *valuing*. All these parts inter-connect, and they all over-lap, so nothing can happen in any one part without affecting the others.

> If I feel aggrieved I will think negatively, behave
> negatively, and under-value the one who has pained
> me; yet if I feel pleased, I am likely to think positively,
> behave constructively, and give high value to the one
> who has pleased me.

Care must be taken not to limit each part too narrowly. For instance, it is sometimes unrealistic to try to separate the things to do with the mind (thinking) from things to do with the soma (feeling); and it is a mistake to confine things of the spirit to the constrictions of what is popularly called 'religion', or religious practices. Anything in which we invest value or worth goes into this area – 'worth-ship' is the same as 'worship'.

Figure 3. **Wholeness**

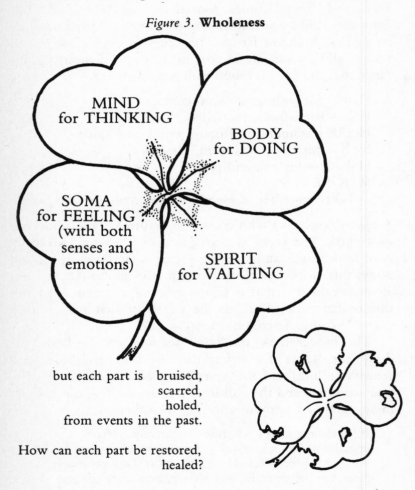

but each part is bruised,
scarred,
holed,
from events in the past.

How can each part be restored,
healed?

Here are other notes to make on Figure 3:

- ☐ no part is more important than any other;
- ☐ each part is bruised and dented, these are the hang-ups left over from earlier stages in our personal history;
- ☐ each part needs space to be exercised and stretched and developed;
- ☐ any part can be affected by stress;
- ☐ we each tend to concentrate on one part rather than another, so the others are apt to lose strength and wither. The whole then becomes distorted, and vulnerable to stress.

This figure can be useful in helping me sort out the shape of my own wholeness.

WHAT USE IS THIS IDEA OF WHOLENESS?

If wholeness is the balanced development of all the parts of ourselves, look at examples of what could happen if we allow an imbalance to develop;

This would be someone who has the body beautiful but who has sacrificed their social contacts, their emotional sensitivity, and their understanding of the world around them in order to achieve it.

This would be someone who is learned and intelligent, but whose health is neglected and who has few friends.

This would be someone who lets their personal feelings take precedence over everything else. Their ungoverned mood-swings impose themselves on all those around them.

This would be someone who rates the spiritual life as something apart from ordinary living; whose head is so high in the clouds that they lose contact with the lives of other people, and lose their sympathy also.

These are caricatures, but they may serve to illustrate how this figure can be useful in imaginatively 'shaping' the way that wholeness works, and how distortions can happen.

Another way of using the idea is in planning goals, making sure projects and plans work out without too much stress.

Take for instance, the garden.

> I am becoming increasingly stressed by the fact that my garden is overrun with weeds, and some rather critical friends are coming to visit me. I only have limited time (and energy) and I want to make sure that I make the most use of what I've got.
> Referring to the wholeness image therefore:
> I use *thinking* to check I have the proper garden tools;
> I use *feeling* (my anxiety) to get myself going and actually enjoy the job;
> I use *doing* to do the work, taking care not to overstrain my back muscles or damage my hands;
> I use my *valuing* because I know it's all worthwhile.

Perhaps most important of all, I must take on board the fact that if I do something else it will be out of *my choice* to do so. Once I accept that something is *my choice*, I can no longer complain that the garden is not tidier, nor can I pretend I should really like it to be different.

This theme is explored in chapter 8. If I take charge of my choice in any matter, the stress attached to it immediately becomes easier to bear. In this case, if I can accept that it is my choice to attend to something other than the garden, I cannot complain. I have made that choice. How to decide between priorities comes later.

HOW DO I RECOGNIZE MY OWN WHOLENESS?

We each have our own special and unique shape, but we each have to find out what that shape is for ourselves. No one can tell us from outside what it is to be Me, although we are influenced strongly by the way others react to our personal behaviour.

The only way for me to find out my own shape is to try it out and see what happens – see how I feel and how others feel about it too. It really means experimenting with the different parts of myself, testing the various weaknesses and strengths that are in me. Others may suggest that doing something this way or that way would be good; but until I have tried it out for myself I will not know whether it is good for me.

What is it that *confirms* me? – makes me most fulfilled and real? I will have to stretch this way and that, discovering things about myself and other people, until I can truly find my own individual shape. For most people this is not an instant discovery; it takes a lifetime.

One of the most obvious, and yet the most difficult, lessons to learn is that *everyone's capacity is different*. We will insist on comparing ourselves with each other 'if he/she/you can do it, so can I'. This comparing of my shape with yours can be a cause of great personal stress. Within certain bounds, this stress can be used to motivate us, that is if we are really made up of similar stuff to the other person; but too often we are not, and we are devaluing ourselves if we persist in pushing ourselves into someone else's mould. We each have our own individual mould to fill and there is no one else who can fit my mould as well as I can, and no one else who can fit yours as well as you can.

So if I am to be wary of comparisons, how am I to discover my own capacity? Figure 4 has proved helpful in

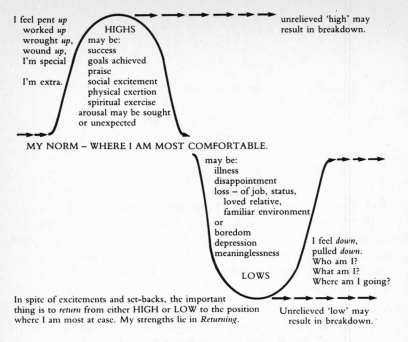

Figure 4. **How do I recognize me?**

illustrating how after each *stretch* of ourselves, after each excursion into a 'high' or a 'low', we return to a place where we feel at home and comfortable. *However much I push and experiment, there is a level at which I can recognize myself as being 'at ease'.* If I stay at that level always, I might well get bored or apathetic, but it is the level to which I must return for my overall balance.

Sometimes I might be very high – excited, stimulated, elated, full of myself; at others I might be very low – disappointed, dispirited, disheartened. After either of these experiences it is important to take steps to regain the 'norm', the place where I am at ease. In order to do this, stress-skills are valuable.

Recognizing my ups and downs and what causes them, helps me to get to know my own capacity. Remember, the same charge of electricity which can work effectively and powerfully through a 13 amp fuse will blow a 5 amp or 3 amp fuse. Which sort am I? Should I keep out of the way of strong currents or do they light me up? I can only find out by trying and noting the consequences.

AWARENESS EXERCISE

Hold in your mind imaginary pictures of two separate people. One person has all the desirable things in life. He has never had a day's illness in his life; he has a large house with money and staff to run it, and all the comfort he could wish for; he has no relationship problems because he has no family and few people can reach through his self-protection; he has no apparent stresses and he makes sure nothing gets to him to upset him. He thinks he has found the answer to a trouble-free existence.

The other person has a very mixed life. She gets overtired sometimes because, with a largish family, she has had to care for a variety of people through bouts of difficulty and illness. Her relationships seem to survive in spite of personal differences and even seem to thrive on contrasts. There has never been quite enough money or comfort or quiet, but nonetheless things have been managed. The family seem to have grown strong, although there have been some major tragedies – one of which resulted in chronic disability. They have experienced some triumphs too. Now in her middle years, the mother has a certain serenity which embraces both the good and the bad times; and people always feel warmer for having met her.

Just keep these two people apart for a while, but hold them together in time. Let them gel in separate corners of your mind . . . Now, to which would you most likely fit the word 'whole'?

———CHRISTIAN OUTLOOK———

Our Lord is recorded in some translations of the gospels as saying, 'Be ye perfect even as your Father in heaven is perfect.' It can be argued that this particular translation is responsible for a great deal of well-meant over-striving, and that this has resulted in much stressful damage.

There has been a considerable amount of research which demonstrates that those personalities who insist on 'perfectionism' are the very ones that are not only vulnerable to stress but who also suffer from the most harmful effects of stress. It is this sort of dis-stress that is most likely to be translated into dis-ease. Those who never give in, never let up, seldom laugh, and seldom play can also become intolerant, moralistic, judgemental and even stricter at pushing themselves than they appear to be with others. Is this the kind of person Our Lord wants us to be when he said, 'Be ye perfect . . .'?

Some authorities have said that Our Lord's words might be translated better as, 'Be ye WHOLE, even as your Father in heaven is WHOLE (but obviously a different sized whole!). It's as if we were being told to fill out, or unfold, our own small individual whole shape in the same way as God the Creator fills out and unfolds his whole vast creation. This is rather more comprehensible than the command to reach a similar state of perfection as God our Father.

Jesus Christ also said, along the same lines, 'Why do you ask me about goodness? What is Good? only your Father in Heaven is good.' He knows we can never be perfect, that we can never be totally 'good'. But we can still work towards becoming WHOLE. Not only can we work towards filling out our own whole, the actual process of doing so balances away the distorting effects of stress, while making use of the motivating effects of stress. So wholeness encompasses stress, just as Jesus Christ did.

'Be ye whole, even as your Father in heaven is whole.'

6
Listening

Up to this point wholeness and the causes and signs of stress have been discussed chiefly from the point of view of *recognition*. In this chapter it is *relating* and *releasing* that will be explored. From here on it is the practical steps that can be taken to get stress to work for you rather than against you that will form the chief emphasis of the book.

A person suffering from stress primarily wants to be listened to. Having recognized the problem, they want to relate it in two ways: to relate the problem to its sources, and to tell someone else about it. Both of these steps involve being listened to, and listening.

Listening isn't always as simple as one might expect. Hopefully, having been listened to, the person under stress will feel better; but in addition, the same person may find that listening to someone else is itself strengthening. If they have been feeling undervalued and stressed, the fact that they themselves have listened and have been of use to another person will build up their sense of competence. The experience of being properly understood is immensely freeing to the one who is being listened to, but equally the experience of properly understanding is immensely affirming to the one who has been doing the listening.

This chapter will look at a number of different forms of listening. These can be charted as in Figure 5.

Each of these ways of listening will be touched upon in the next few pages. To start with, *How I can listen to You?* There are volumes describing the various arts of the different ways of listening, but the essential bones are in the following summary:

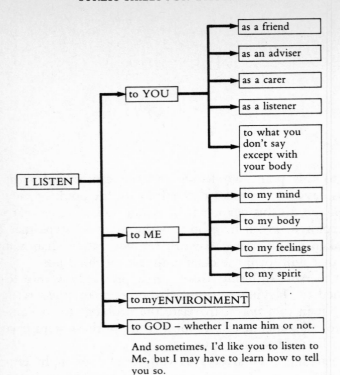

And sometimes, I'd like you to listen to Me, but I may have to learn how to tell you so.

Figure 5. **Types of Listening**

1. The listening of a *Friend*
   is rather like *building a staircase:*
   each takes turns at listening and talking;
   each adds something of their own point of view;
   each adds something of their own experience;
   there is equally free expression;
   each shares the responsibility of building up the friendship.

2. The listening of an *Adviser*
   is rather like *setting a compass:*
   the talking is one-sided, the adviser mostly listens;
   the adviser seldom adds from his own experience, unless he is specifically asked for it;

the adviser is not allowed free expression, this is for the talker only;

the adviser does not interrupt, except when it is necessary to clarify a situation;

the adviser carries the responsibility for a satisfactory outcome, usually by suggesting, as a conclusion, an appropriate course to follow.

3. The listening of a *Carer*
is rather like *offering a warm armchair:*
the talking is largely one-sided, the carer encouraging the the talker to express his feelings;

the carer avoids comparing experiences or points of view, he does not say, 'I know just how you feel';

the carer's role is to be supportive, not critical, providing reassurance such as, 'You're doing fine. You're great where you are. We can get more help when you feel you need it;

the carer takes the responsibility of leaving the talker feeling more confident.

4. The listening of a *Listener*
is rather like *erecting scaffolding:*
the talking is one-sided, the listener limiting himself to the odd 'grunt' to encourage free expression the talker (such sounds can include 'ah' or 'er' but not 'O!');

the listener accepts, unconditionally, everything that the talker needs to spill over, registering it only with reponses which use, as far as possible, the words and emotions of the talker himself; as he 'reflects' these, the listener may be able to bolster the insights of the talker in unforeseen ways. If this happens, then the responsibility for the positive outcome has been properly shared.

For really caring listening there are certain things to attend to, and things to avoid.

The things to concentrate on are:

- [ ] *offering the talker warmth*; try to really get inside what they are saying, without being dragged down by it.
- [ ] *being prepared to meet his eye* whenever the talker looks for it. A staring gaze can be off-putting, but let the talker take his eyes away from yours rather than you taking yours away from his.
- [ ] *belief that what he is saying is the truth for him* at that moment as he sees it. Maybe you will have to sort out some of the 'ifs' and 'buts' later, but not while he is talking.
- [ ] *allowing the talker to express negative feelings*. Often a hand on an arm or shoulder, or holding in a good hug, can convey without words more understanding than long speeches.
- [ ] *emphasizing that whatever happens*, even if it is 'the worst', there will be somebody or something around to lean on. Perhaps you can help work out how this would be in practice.
- [ ] *using his words* to make sure you have understood his meaning; sometimes phrases such as, 'It sounds as if you are feeling pretty mad/hurt/upset/left out/put down/cheated,' can help to convince him you have grasped his point.
- [ ] *allowing him to see his own connections* between things; as he talks the speaker may see things in a different light and come to new conclusion himself.
- [ ] *observe what is not said as much as what is said* (see Figure 5).

The things to avoid are:

- [ ] *interrupting*, even if you are clear about what you are being told. Interruptions can be very damaging to spontaneous 'flow'.
- [ ] *direct questioning*, especially 'why' questions; these can be particularly threatening. Try to frame necessary queries into 'I wonder if . . .?' or 'I don't know how . . .?' or 'What do you think would happen if . . .?'
- [ ] *bland reassurance*; the phrases, 'I know it's going to be all

right,' and, 'I feel just the same as you,' and, 'The same thing happened to me,' may be comforting to the one who says them but they are patently not true. It is even condescending to expect the other to be reassured by them.

☐ *filling in gaps* in the conversation too quickly. The speaker may be gathering his thoughts or his energy, and will not want to be diverted. Continue to attend quietly while he collects himself.

☐ *framing your next remark* while he is still speaking. Probably all that will be needed is an encouraging grunt or monosyllable; he will soon know if you are thinking about your words rather than his.

☐ *forming judgements*; never express your opinion unless it is directly asked, and even then guard against sounding unsympathetic. Gentleness and warmth are the most releasing responses to offer someone in distress.

☐ *giving advice!* But there are rare occasions when phrases like, 'Sometimes it can help if . . .' or, 'Others have told me that . . .' can help the person find his own pathway and make his own decision.

Listening to what is *not* said is as important as listening to what is put into words. In trying to absorb the meaning that the other person *intends* rather than the one his words exactly *express* we can be helped by learning to read the special language of our bodies. It has been claimed that as much as two-thirds of what we communicate to each other is made up of signals that do not use words; so the messages are non-verbal. The body-language examples below indicate some of the ways our bodies send messages. But these are only examples; in practice the signs are infinitely more variable, and our bodies give out nuances and subtleties that are barely possible to frame in words. So don't take these ideas as being always literal or as applying to all situations; they are merely a guide.

BODY LANGUAGE EXAMPLES

When listening carefully observe the following:

The HEAD –
  What statement is in the hairstyle?
    Is it reserved/flamboyant?
    Is it well groomed/neglected?
    What care is taken of the hair condition?
  What statement is in the tilt of the head?
    Head held back may be the result of military training,
      or it may be showing a feeling of defensiveness.
    Head held at a sideways angle may indicate
      deference, or insecurity, or self-reserve.
    Head held with chin out indicates some aggression –
      the owner is a go-getter, an achiever.
      With chin in could mean the owner is judgemental.
      With chin up could mean the owner feels superior.
      With chin down could mean the owner is depressed.
    Head held straight and poised indicates that the owner
      is assured and balanced.

The FACE –
  Is it forced or natural?
  Are the eyes masked or open? If the pupils are widely
    dilated it means the owner is aroused.
  Are the eyelids hooded with apathy or wide-open with
    wonder?
  Are the forehead creases deep and habitual, or are they
    mobile and constantly changing?
  Where are they? Crows' feet around the eyes from
    smiling? or between the eyebrows from frowning?
  Is the mouth drawn tight, or is it relaxed? The tiny
    circular muscles around the mouth, are they easy and
    flexible, or stiff and un-giving?
  Is the smile ready, or slow, or sincere, or formal?
  Suppressed stress will give itself away by twitches in
    the face, minute spasms of muscle about the eyelids or

nose or mouth.
Stress can also result in a loss of movement and variety in expression.

The VOICE –

Excitement and stress are soon registered in the vocal cords which control the voice. Listen to its pitch and timbre as well as listening to the speed and sound of the words.

The SHOULDERS –

Stress-signs are very well known in the shoulders.
Are they raised, taut, hunched, or lowered and relaxed?
Are they rounded, self-protective, and defensive?
Are they held back, determined and rigid?
Do they look overburdened? Do they cope with the 'weight' put upon them?

The ARMS –

may be loosely swinging, easy, enjoying their freedom, or may be held close to the body, tense, closed, guarded.

The HANDS –

may be open, receptive, accepting what comes, or may be closed, fearful/aggressive, forming a fist.
Are the nails well cared for? bitten? out of condition?
Are fingers twitching, or stroking themselves for comfort?

The TRUNK –

Is it upright, balanced, alert?
Is it slumped, curved, dejected?
Is it bent forward at the hips, anxiously trying to get 'there'?
Is it unbending and stiff and inflexible?

The PELVIS –

Is it held in a horizontal balance? or tilted sideways, (which may result in pain elsewhere)?
Is it held back protectively, tipped forward invitingly?

Do the hips move easily when walking?

The LEGS –
When sitting, are they crossed tightly and insecure?
or held gracefully?
Are the open knees challenging or accepting?
Do the feet swing anxiously?

GESTURE and GAIT –
Do these seem competent or wanting to impress?
confident or frantic?
sleepy, apathetic, hurried, or relaxed?

These are only some indications of how a body 'talks'; they cannot be applied always or universally, but they can show us ways in which we can begin to guess at the tensions the other person is having to deal with.

★   ★   ★   ★   ★

Some of the worst non-physical violence we can do to another human being is not to listen to them. To withdraw interest, to ignore them as if there was no one there; to deny them the warmth and attention they need is a powerful put-down. Yet we do it to ourselves all the time.

When did you last sit down and listen, really LISTEN, to *yourself*? Listening to others is of enormous importance, and with the emphasis today on the use of counselling skills, more and more people are becoming aware of the skills of positive listening; yet we rarely apply these to ourselves. The attentiveness of the listening we offer others will actually be improved if we have first paused to hear what is going on inside ourselves.

LISTENING TO MYSELF – to my MIND

Inside my head there is a continuous patter going on. Often it is the parent in me urging on the child; or it may be the child protesting at what is being asked of it; or it can be the adult in me weighing up the pros and cons of what I'm planning to do. Generally during my working hours, I don't listen consciously to what is happening inside. I'm too busily distracted by what I have in hand at present. But until I do listen I can neither know nor change it, and much of it does need changing! Sometimes it is as though the needle on a record has got stuck, and I find I am repeating over and over again phrases and responses that I have brought with me from the past and never developed. I may discover that I turn on the automatic reaction too unthinkingly, when it isn't the best approach. If I listen, I can break into these habitual repetitions and take them in hand. It may be that they could be made more constructive, working for me and others rather than against us. How?

Listening-in to my 'SELF-TALK' need not be a difficult task. Once I am aware of what is going on I can tune in during any routine task, and apply just the same ways of not interrupting and questioning that I would use when listening intently to someone else. When the clamour within me becomes more familiar, I can begin to recognize how it influences my daily behaviour, and point out to myself all the calculating little tricks I use to get what I want – or at least what I thought I wanted. All the twists I put on circumstances to work them in my favour, as if I had to prove something against somebody else all the time. *(By the way, who is this Bogey who seems to be trying to get me down all the time? Is he really there?)* Examining it all a bit more truthfully and maturely will show me how to sort some of it out:

☐ sort out how much of the response I commonly use is based on good experience, and how much on bad, unreliable experience;

☐ sort out how much of it is really based on reason rather than fantasy;

☐ sort out how much is emotional and shows how deeply I really feel, and how much is a 'put up job' just to get my way;

☐ sort out useful intuitions and misguided apprehensions;

□ sort out what actually works effectively, and what
   doesn't;
□ sort out what I carry from the past and which is no
   longer appropriate, and which needs updating;
□ sort out where I'm going and if I really want to go
   there after all or not;
□ sort out which bits of my responses are to do with
   the 'role' I have in life, and which are really as I want
   them to be,

This sorting exercise is particularly necessary when I
know I am under stress and realize something has to be re-
ordered. If awareness has become a frequent exercise it will
greatly add to the strength of my coping skills in times of
special stress or crisis.

When I listen to my mind, I can start to imprint upon
it, quite deliberately, some of the tactics I have learned to
trust through observation. These will include little
'formulas', short-cuts, that have been shaped out of my
experience, my reason, the demands made upon me, my

priorities, and most of all through knowing my own capabilities. So I can tone down those words and actions of mine
which I recognize tend to make things worse, such as:

My self-talk says, angrily,
    'He *never* . . . offers to meet me', or
    'They *always* . . . expect me to . . .';
    but both reason and experience lead me to defuse these
      statements so they become
    'He *sometimes* doesn't meet me', and
    'They *often* expect me to . . .'.

My self-talk says peevishly,
    'I *must* visit my mother-in-law', or
    '*No one* understands me';
    but in the light of the demands made upon me and my
      own priorities they become
    'I *will try* to visit my mother-in-law', and
    'Well, she does understand me *a bit*'.

My self-talk says unrealistically,
    'My boss *has to* have this whole report typed on his desk
      tomorrow';
    but in view of my own capability I can adjust my attitude
      into
    'Would he prefer half the amount done in the
      time or the whole amount done in double
      the time? I'll ask him'.

LISTENING TO MY BODY

Listening to my body myself is a skill that is only beginning
to be re-established in our society. Ever since we put aside
a section of our population to specialize – and prosper – in
medicine and health care, people have tended to put the
responsibility of listening to their bodies into the hands of
someone else. The interpretation of cries of pain from our
bodies certainly needs the help of professionals and the highly

technological equipment they have developed; but there are simpler, quieter messages sent to warn us of strain and it is these that we often don't hear. It is when we remain consistently deaf to the gentler clues that crises build up and the whispers become cries. For instance:

☐ Listen to my *breathing:*
   Is it easy, effortless, and relaxed?
☐ Listen to my *heart-beat:*
   Is it comforting, steady, reassuring?

☐ Listen to my *stomach:*
   Is it settled, satisfied, neither bloated nor tight?

☐ Listen to my *senses:*
   What are my ears hearing, *now?* How far can they hear?
   What are my eyes observing, *now?* How much detail are they taking in? Are they tired or sore?
   What can I taste? Do I take time to taste, or am I too busy anticipating the next mouthful?
   What am I smelling? Does smell help me to remember and associate things?
   What am I touching? Is touching nice? Is it something I enjoy, or something I avoid?

☐ Listen to my *muscles:*
   What makes them ache? which parts of my body are easy and comfortable *now?*
   Which muscles are taut and prepared for action that doesn't happen?

☐ Listen to my *neck, shoulders, back, and feet* especially.
   These areas carry a lot of weight, literally and metaphorically. If I hear them clearly, I can begin to gauge how well they are carrying the weight – or burden – that is upon me. Listen well.

Our bodies send warnings of stress in the form of tiredness, irritability, headaches, jangling nerves, aching muscles, interrupted sleep, queer pains, bunged-up or over-active bowels, or sensitive bladders that need constant relief. All these signs can be overridden, and often are, by our free use of caffeine, nicotine, alcohol, tranquillizers and stimulants to get us through our day. No wonder the physical signs get blunted, and our doctors and hospitals are kept well occupied.

LISTENING TO MY FEELINGS

The skills of owning my feelings have been greatly emphasized this century. Allowing myself to be me has been discussed in the previous chapter, but perhaps it would be appropriate here to add a note on 'how *much*' to listen to my feelings? The desire to know everything about myself can be very great; myself may be fascinating to me, and one can become totally absorbed by the study. No doubt we all at some stage would like to know that the knots we find within ourselves have been fully untangled. However, if it has taken a few decades to produce those knots, it will surely take just as long to unravel them totally. Sometimes I will just have to accept that they are there, and part of the shape that is me, and I will have to go ahead with my life using the shape I am. If I continue striving too hard for too long for a shape that is not me – however perfect I would like it to be – I will not even be able to cope with what I am. Accepting and using the NOW, the platform I have reached HERE from which to go forward, may be a better thing than forever pursuing a search backward into how I came to reach it.

LISTENING TO MY SPIRIT

Later in this book the subject of listening to the things of the spirit will be enlarged. At this stage it is worth pointing out that it is what we value that constructs the framework that either supports us or lets us down when we are feeling stressed. The stronger and more realistic our values are, the stronger and more realistic our life support will be. So whatever it is that we put worth into, we will lean on that when we are feeling empty or lost. It may be the values of a specific ethic or religion, but it may be material values of things, or the values of family or sport or animals or politics or caring for others. As long as we are aware of what our values are, and we take time to listen to them, we may be safe from meaninglessness. It is the listening to them that is crucial, for that is the only way we can discover whether they are in fact strong enough to support us. And more, whether they would be strong enough to hold us steady in times of crisis and acute stress.

LISTENING TO MY ENVIRONMENT

Being aware of and listening to my environment is all part of knowing my capabilities. Recognizing things about the area where I live which cause stress to me and others is the first step to doing anything about easing the situation. Places of work and recreation can affect the people who spend time there by either stressing or rewarding them, and which way it goes very often will depend upon how they manage the circumstances. Later chapters go into the ways of changing circumstances, managing time, making decisions, and reducing the jags in our lives, but it all starts with listening to things around us.

LISTENING TO GOD

People are always asking, 'How do I listen to God?' One can hardly know if there is a God, or what God is like, if he/she is never listened to. Is it possible to set time aside to *listen*, not talk or ask or tell or even praise, but just *listen* without interruption and without questioning, to find out what God there is and what he is like? It's worth bearing this question at the back of your mind for a while, before reaching chapter 10. How and when and where will be looked at a bit more closely later on, with the discussion on erecting a space and on affirmation.

GETTING OTHERS TO LISTEN TO ME

It's all very well my listening to others and listening to me and listening to God, but sometimes the pressure cooker has to let off steam if it is not going to explode, and I have to get someone to listen to *me*.

Sometimes 'telling trouble halves a trouble'. So how can we persuade others – who themselves may be busy or troubled and pre-occupied – to listen to us? One way is to seek out a professional counsellor, or you may be lucky and have exactly the right friend at hand. But there are many occasions when a 'suitable' listener with 'suitable' time doesn't seem to be available, and a certain strategy has to be used to persuade someone to listen. Here are some ideas of how to approach such a situation:

A needs to off-load, to be listened to, and he would like B to be the person to whom he could talk. But B is busy:

> A explains his need without adding any emotional content; B will be more ready to respond to a straightforward request than to a demand which tastes of moral coercion? For instance:

> 'There is something important to me that I'd like to talk to you about. Can I tell you? It is in a bit of a muddle so please let me get it out without stopping, or I might lose the thread.'

> *or*: 'Could you spare me some time? Can we sit down? / go outside a minute? / move into another room?' (suggesting a 'natural break' shows that the matter is important to you).

X should offer understanding about Y's position, as well as asking for understanding of her own, so a little negotiation can help. For instance:

'I realize this is an awkward moment right now, because you are making the supper / worried because it's late / deep in the telly – but could I have some of your time later if I do the washing-up now?'

or: 'Let's go out for a cup of coffee – I very much want to hear how you got on at . . . and there's something I'd like to ask your advice about too. Have you enough time before the children come home? Can I treat you?'

AN AWARENESS EXERCISE

Do you have a friend or member of your family you can agree to share this with? Take any page of this chapter, read it together, determine a particular time you can give to trying out the suggestions on that page, and then compare notes with each other about what it meant to you – or not. The whole chapter is about exercising awareness, but to make it real it's not only the reading about it that explains it, but actual practice. Agreeing to do it with someone else means the practice gets done, and your experience will be enlarged.

It has been a long chapter, but then, whichever way you look at it, *Listening is the starting point* to everything else.

Listening involves waiting, watching, attending. Is there a better definition of prayer?

————CHRISTIAN OUTLOOK————

The older translations of the New Testament have some phrases we now just roll off our tongues without thinking. Such as 'and he answered and said unto them . . .' He *answered* necessarily implies that Jesus Christ had first *listened!*

Time and time again we read that Jesus acted in response to somebody; that is, that he listened first and then acted. Knowing all things and understanding all people, he still knew it to be worthwhile and worth the effort to listen to what they had to say before he responded. Listening gives the other person value, worth, dignity. Not talking while they are talking says they are significant, worthy of attention; Jesus knew that to presume you know what the other wants to say before they have said it is deflating and diminishing.

Jesus Christ listens, then and now.

There are many instances in the gospel when Jesus is recorded as listening before talking or doing. Most of his teaching was in the form of question (which commonly involves listening) and answer. According to the *Modern Concordance to the New Testament* (DLT 1976) there are 923 usages of the word in this way, and in addition there are pages and pages specifying texts which include the words 'listen' and 'hear'. For our purposes here, consider the way he listened to the Roman centurion (Luke 7:1–10), the Syro-Phoenician woman (Mark 7:24–30), the Samaritan woman at the well (John 4:7–26), Martha and Mary at Lazarus's grave (John 11:20–45), or the story of the father of the boy with a dumb spirit (Mark 9:14–29). In all these cases the gospels record Jesus as listening *before* he did what he must have known he had to do from the outset of the meeting. He listens patiently, never presuming to know what they are about to say. He gives time and total attention to the speaker, because Jesus is a master at listening. He also wanted his hearers to express what their need was. He used to listen to the answer to his question, 'what would you have me to do?' He still does.

Jesus listens with infinite compassion, but his compassion isn't woolly. He could be pointedly direct too. He has another frequent remark, which he delivered with great realism, and it still strikes deep:

'Listen, those of you who have ears to hear . . .'

Have we?

7
Allowing

This is a very important chapter, and it is about things that don't come easily. There are two areas of ourselves that none of us are very good at; yet if we deny either, it increases our stress. One area is that of allowing ourselves bad feelings, and the other is allowing ourselves rewards.

We all have, inside us, a great number of things we won't allow. If we freed ourselves inside a bit more, the prohibitions that come at us from outside wouldn't be so irksome. Becoming conscious of stress gives us the opportunity for looking at the dark inside things which cause such strong reactions. This can be uncomfortable, because obviously we dislike recognizing in ourselves things we don't like; in fact more often than not we put these on to other people and then are content that they should take the blame for them. Some of the things we least like are those 'survival' emotions that stress itself arouses: fear, self-doubt, inferiority, anger, resentment, aggression, bravado are among those that are least comfortable. We avoid owning them, just like we jokingly avoid owning our children when they are muddy and naughty – only this is no joke. It's for real, we don't want to acknowledge that such disagreeable emotions live within us.

Often it is our own behaviour, our own reactions to stress, that leave us as much stressed as the original stressor. Until we acknowledge this, and allow that our irritableness and bad temper, our irresponsibility and self-indulgence, may in fact be a mask for deeper feelings of inadequacy, insecurity, self-disgust, or boredom, nothing much will change. One student looked at his 'terror of being found out' before he could allow that the phoney over-confidence which he hid behind produced more stress in him than the original fear. Until we allow ourselves to feel what we'd rather not feel, we can't know what it is that we do feel – only what we feel we *ought to feel*.

> If I peel away the disguises under which I commonly
> hide myself and accept the darker side of me, allow that
> it exists, I can then take meaures to deal with it. I need
> to be really honest with myself: I'd like to deny that
> I'm scared, or scarred, or that I am holding on to anger
> and resentment, or that I'm still hugging a conviction
> I've always been hard done by, or that I feel I've always
> been emotionally swindled. I'm really not very nice.
> But unless I do admit these things I can't take a
> sufficiently good look at them to discover that the fears
> are possibly unfounded, or that the resentment can be
> released, or the imbalance can be re-set. I have to give
> permission to myself to be myself before I can do
> anything to fundamentally change myself. Then I can
> develop skills to cope with my stress.

★ ★ ★ ★ ★

How we feel and think very often controls what we DO. It's as if we treat our strong emotions like wild animals that are uncontrollable until they are caged and cramped. In case they unexpectedly get out we surround them with prohibitions, with 'don'ts' and 'mustn'ts'. This wariness of our own emotions is fed by a very basic need we all have of being approved; as children, we discovered that the easiest and simplest way of getting approval was to do as we were told. The child in us still wants to gain approval by obeying the rules, so we bolster ourselves and our sense of 'rightness' with 'do's' and 'don'ts' all the way. We feel safe within familiar boundaries laid out for us by the conditioning we had in childhood. Much of our social behaviour is kept in control by these rules and boundaries, and those things that are uncomfortable or don't fit in are buried underground. The strange thing is, that the harder we *strive* to keep within

these rules (whether they are imposed on us from others, or whether we impose them on ourselves by our own attempts at perfectionism), so the likelihood of becoming stressed increases.

Allowing means giving permission, saying to ourselves, 'You may admit to these feelings,' and then taking responsibility for what happens. Ad-mitting, letting-in our disagreeable feelings does not mean giving ourselves permission to let them out again on to other people: what it does mean is that we take conscious control of them and deal with something nearer to the truth than the fantasy of what we are.

It means allowing the pieces of ourselves we don't want and we don't like and we don't admit to, to actually BE. It is when we have allowed that they exist that we can take charge of them, rather than cramping them so tight inside that they break out and take control of us. That can land us in the state that is graphically called 'break-down'.

An added difficulty about keeping nasties under and not acknowledging them, is that with them we also bury all sorts of goodies. If we are prepared to take the nasties in hand, it's reasonable that we should also accept the goodies and not reject the rewards. Self-negation and 'selflessness' have been so built into our Christian culture, that it can come hard to some people to affirm rewards. If we don't, the denial of them can 'turn' (like good milk that turns sour) into self-pity.

Un-burying these goodies sometimes needs an effort; arousing the awareness of the pleasurable things around us can be difficult when we have become used to ignoring them. Our English culture is peculiarly strict about keeping the hatches down when we are feeling *glad;* sometimes it seems more acceptable to show that we are feeling bad or mad (eccentric 'mad dogs and Englishmen') than that we are actually feeling glad. Another strange thing about those rewards that we find for ourselves is this: those that come from outside, a new possession perhaps, can bring very great pleasure but often this pleasure has a surprisingly short life; those things we find pleasure in for ourselves seem to be self-perpetuating and are more likely to be available always.

Of course, if we are to appreciate our own rewards, we must make sure that others who are close to us are rewarded too. Whether their choice of rewards is the same as ours is neither here nor there, but it is our business to see that they get the rewards *they* want. Sometimes, and best of all, we will be able to share them together, and a shared pleasure is the best of all.

The word 'reward' conjures up prizes: a pay rise, a status house, an exotic holiday. Rather than these, here it means the sharp pleasure which we can get without any cost to others – it doesn't even demand their attention or involvement. So others need not bear the burden of rewarding us, of continually telling us we're O.K. It means becoming aware of things with which I can reward myself, which can become part of my own shape and privacy, without tediously depending on someone else's approval. We can all find our own, but these are some that have been suggested:

    clean socks;
    cool breeze on the skin;
    chuckling;
    watching clouds;
    sucking ice;
    stroking an animal;
    tastes on the tongue;
    people contact;
    bare feet on green grass;
    a hot bath with a hot drink and a good book;
    admiring the cake I made myself;
    basking, in sunlight or firelight or whatever; just basking;
    feeling the power and movement in my own muscles;
    pleasure in giving pleasure – waving at the postman;
    pleasure in shapes, colours, textures, words, music, making-up, friends, using my hands, feeling good, watching moths, quietness, chatter,

the list is endless . . .

Too often we feel paupered, deprived, self-pitying, because we aren't offered sufficient appreciation; and yet we forget to take note of the wealth of instant rewards we can give ourselves if only we allow ourselves to do so! Becoming conscious of the 'hurrahs!' in our lives can help to balance the 'horrors' of which we are more aware. If recognition is the first of the stress-skills, allowing ourselves rewards for having shouldered our bad feelings must come a close second.

★   ★   ★   ★   ★

This may be a good point for a little anecdote. It is a good illustration of how we can actually put ourselves in the way of receiving rewards, when we feel we are in need of them.

A young mother with three small children had worked

hard all day amusing them while the school was on
holiday and Dad was away on a business trip. She was
tired and drained, and knew she had to summon up the
energy to prepare the evening meal and get them all to
bed without too much fretfulness. All she wanted to do
was to rest. So she gathered all the bits and pieces of old
make-up that she could find, and cream, and brushes
and combs and called the children into her bedroom.
Then she said 'I'm going to lie on the bed, and you can
do anything you like to me while I keep my eyes shut.
You can clean my face with cream, and then put on
any colours you like anyhow you like. When I open my
eyes and look in the mirror, what will I see? A witch
or a fairy-queen?' . . .

   The children had a marvellous time using their
imagination, and mother had a 'rest' while the gentle
fingers of the little girls played over her face and hair.
And they all felt rewarded.

★　★　★　★　★

In sorting out what I honestly feel, and what I feel I ought
to feel, it can be a useful exercise to imagine the parent, the
child, and the adult who co-exist within me. Sometimes I
can recognize the parent inside me nagging at the child who
lives there too, and the child wheedling and manipulating
the parent. Then it's time for the more mature *adult* in me
to persuade the *parent* and the *child* to see each other's point
of view and come to terms with each other's existence, even
to make friends with each other. Then we can live together
as a trio instead of a three-party conflict.

> If my parent/child/adult viewpoints are all arguing within
> me about how I should behave, I shall be jangling and
> fragmented and highly stressed; if however my parent/
> child/adult come together sharing an appreciation of the
> different roles I give them, I shall be tingling and whole
> and highly rewarded.

★　★　★　★　★

What of the strong feelings surrounding sex, are they to be
allowed, permitted? Of course! Once feelings are allowed,

decisions can be taken about what to do with them, that are appropriate to the situation. In relation to the state of stress, there is a difference between the feelings aroused in a crisis, and those experienced in habitual or continual stress. In a real crisis feelings of sex become irrelevant. Faced with a dinosaur the desire to reproduce his kind would have deserted the cave-man. Generally acute fear ousts sex. However where there is continual pressure in everyday life, sexual feelings can go either way: the desire for sex – particularly casual, frequent, or even violent sex – may be a distraction and a means of proving one's doubted capability; alternatively, the continued stress may be so draining that even fundamental cravings seep away.

> When I am really stressed what I most need is a sexual partner who can be tender and in-filling rather than one who is demanding and emptying. When my partner understands this need, caring bodily love is not only a buffer to stress, but it consoles and builds and strengthens the best that is in me.

★　★　★　★　★

How does all this work out in practice? What happens after I have allowed those feelings in myself that make me sad, bad or glad? It may be useful to summarize what can be done in the form of four suggestions. These can then be used to either trim down or fill out the image I present in real life situations. Instead of having to put up with that image ruling – or even devouring – me, I shall be able to build a bit more of my own control into it. And I can allow something that is closer to the person I should like to be, to show and grow.

1. When I truly know what makes me feel bad, sad, or glad, I can take charge of these thoughts and feelings. The ways in which I can express them and let them out without harming other people are discussed in the next chapter.

2. When I know my own weaknesses I can begin to foresee what is likely to topple me. Do I want to sidestep these situations? or to ask others for help in order to cope with them?

3. When I can read my own reactions, I can start to unravel which of the expectations I put upon myself are realistic, and which are based on fantasy. Perhaps I can then draw the fantasy closer to the reality.

4. When I allow myself to be me, I can recognize how much of my responses are the result of me projecting the things I dislike about myself on to others, and how much is the result of what others project on to me. Sorting that out makes life more bearable for everyone.

For examples, these are real-life stresses identified by students:

☐ 'Someone humiliates me, I respond by hurting them and then feel ashamed and stressed.'

Apply **1**. Allow the hurt, recognize it. Now what to do? Take it out on the one that did the hurting, thereby redoubling the hurt? Or shall I absorb it for the moment and release the tension later by looking at it with a trusted friend? Why did it hurt so much? How could the hurt be healed? There may be ideas in the next chapter that would help.

☐ 'I find my week is far too full and I think about it ALL at once, so I panic.'

Apply **2**. Allow the panic, recognize it, don't bury it. Now, what to do? Look at the diary, and consciously put aside a definite portion of time in which to objectify what there is to be done. Perhaps it will mean getting up 20 minutes earlier one day, or giving up half an hour of TV, but in that time write down all that has to be done and put it into order. A later chapter on 'too many demands' looks at the tactics of setting realistic goals and managing time. See what things don't really have to be done, and what things other people can help with doing.

☐ 'There are too many things I'm expected to do and I have difficulty in refusing, so I get very stressed.'

Apply **3**. Allow the frustration, realize the impractibility of getting it all done. Now, what to do? Sort out quietly what is really necessary to do and what it would be nice to get done in order to prove you can do it. These latter expectations may in fact be things you put upon yourself just 'to show them'. So adjust your ideas of your own capacity, and discuss the reality of the situation calmly with whoever it is who is expecting too much of you. Putting a point of view without arousing negative passions will be discussed again later, together with assertion tactics.

☐ 'What gets me is when the other person won't do the thing in the way I want it done. That gets me very stressed.'

Apply **4**. Allow the feelings of wanting to control, to dominate; don't deny them. Now examine them. Why do you want your own way so badly? Is it actually part of feeling under-valued? What are the advantages of doing it their way? What is positive in the other person's point of view? Try to negotiate, give a point or two and keep a point or two. Choosing to share control comes into 'equipping our children' also.

Now go and reward yourself!

And don't forget to laugh!

You will find out quite a lot by setting yourself an exercise.

AWARENESS EXERCISE

Isn't all this introspection rather selfish? Doesn't it smack of self-gazing? Consider these terms:

self-indulgent	self-sufficient
self-absorbed	self-offering

self-knowledgeable	self-aware
self-denying	self-deprecating
self-assured	self-understanding
self-negating	self-giving
self-centred	self-important

Which of these terms are negative, narcissistic, and tend to keep others out? Which of them are positive, affirming, and tend to let others in?
Which would come under a heading of SELF-CONCEIT?
   – having a fanciful idea of oneself.
Which would come under a heading of SELF-ESTEEM?
   – having a realistic estimation of oneself
   (to estimate means to add up the plusses and minuses).

———CHRISTIAN OUTLOOK———

Did Christ ever say, 'Thou shalt not love thyself'?

Or has self-negation been a misconstrued attitude, and has it encouraged the faithful to remain meek, mild, and obedient?
Christ understood the man who said 'I am Legion' to such a fundamental depth, he knew that only a whole herd of wild pigs would be enough to house the multitude of feelings twisted up inside him. Do I have a legion of feelings inside me? Do I recognise them? The pandemonium within the demoniac was just that – 'pan', meaning many, demons.
Jesus Christ actually said, 'Love thy neighbour *as thyself*,' i.e. in the same way that you should love yourself. Not cosset yourself perhaps, but know and comprehend what is inside you, make friends with it, so that you can better know and comprehend what is likely to be inside your neighbours. *Have I got to love myself and all I find inside myself as well as I try to love my neighbour?* Will I respond to difficulties better if I do?
Christ himself knew about the strong feelings inside him; not only did he recognize them, he also talked about them to others. Unless he had communicated these very interior

feelings to someone else, we would not have had in the gospels vivid accounts of things that happened when he was totally on his own – for instance the temptations in the wilderness and his agony in the garden of Gethsemane.

So we have his example not only in recognizing his own internal tensions, but for relating them, on occasion, as well.

8

Taking charge of my choice

Taking charge of my choice is the keynote of how to 'harmonize' the stress in my life. We all know that stress can cause discord, but with the use of stress-skills this can be resolved. The real question underlying my approach to stress is 'Who calls the tune?' *Can I take charge of my choice?* That is, can I handle stress in such a way that in the end I will be a more whole person, more responsible for my own decisions and my own actions? Or will I still need to blame others and outside issues for the distress in my life?

There is all the difference in the world between feeling I *have* to do something, and actually *choosing* to do it. This chapter is about how to turn those things we feel have been put upon us and which aggravate us into a matter of *choice*. As soon as there is a possible alternative to what I have to do, there comes an opportunity to choose, and if I so want, I can choose to do it differently. And as soon as I have an element of choice, I can take charge of it. With that, I can let go the resentment that hangs on to those things I feel I have to do when I don't want to do them. This chapter will take a look at choice, anger, blame, decision-making and how we tend to project our negative feelings on to others.

To put all that into an example:

I have a demanding elderly relative living with me. She is querulous, forgetful, and unhappy. Her presence reduces me to jelly, and a screaming frustrated jelly at that.

BUT, I have a choice –

either to learn to cope with her demands objectively, with
a detachment that is warm nonetheless;
or to deny/neglect them, but thereby to risk increasing
everyone's misery.

It is my choice

If I *choose* to make the best of things, the stress upon me
will in due course be lessened; if I *choose* to let them get
worse, the stress upon everyone will be worsened. But
I will in fact have *chosen*.

In this instance my choice 'to make the best of things' will
also involve many skills, such as the use of objectivity,
assertion, time management, mobilising help from others,
planning small goals, avoiding the blame-game, among
others. Some of these will have to be learned quite
consciously, so it is by no means an easy choice to make. The
three chapters will deal with most of these very practical issues.

To take another, much simpler, example:

The Smith family always kept their dustbin at the side
of the house, near the back door. The refuse collection
was supposed to be made from there, but the new men
apparently didn't realize that, and the dustbin didn't get
emptied. Mr and Mrs Smith wrote a letter of complaint
to the Council, fretting at their increasing pile of
rubbish, and wailed to the neighbours. 'Why shouldn't
they do it properly? Why should we make it easier for
them? Why should we put up with so much – we can't
sleep for worry.'

The Brown family living next door with the same
arrangements chose to move their dustbin to where it
was more visible for the new men to find it. It was a
slight bother, but at least the rubbish got cleared. In the
long run they spent less energy on hassle and got what
they really wanted in addition. That was their choice.

In taking charge of my choice
  I am not allowing stress to take charge of my life,
  but using the energy of stress to put charge into my life.

★　★　★　★　★

A considerable amount of our daily energy is put into behaviour that we imagine will earn approval. Perhaps I like to think that if people see me as a willing horse who can put up with being 'flogged', then they will say, 'Oh isn't she wonderful!' and I can carry a secret glow. That's fine if that is what I choose to be, but the difficulty comes when I don't get the approval I had hoped for, and then I turn into a 'Poor Little Me!'

Or sometimes I imagine that if I am seen to be ceaselessly busy, someone will say, 'Oh I don't know how she copes!' and come and help me. If that is what I choose and that is how it happens then that's fine, but the difficulty comes when I don't get help, and I won't ask for it, and then I turn into 'Look at Martyrish Me!'

Or sometimes I hide my real strength and let others think I am helpless and weak so that they can think they dominate me. If that is what I choose and the false position can be kept up all may be well, but the difficulty comes when the others find out and I turn myself into 'Mistreated Me!'

If, instead of depending so heavily on others' approval, I chose to be a bit more objective about the true situation and my own position in it, I would actually be less likely to lose their approval. Some of the greatest put-offs are Poor Little Me, Martyrish Me, and Mistreated Me. These are also among our most often adopted poses. How can they be avoided?

By choosing to see things clearly and state things objectively.

By deliberately ferreting out the little tricks and twists, the calculated turns, the devious put-ons we use to set people up and get our own way; by learning how to present things without allowing them to become loaded with unhelpful issues; by using what today is known as *'assertiveness'* (and used to be known as 'objectivity').

★ ★ ★ ★ ★

ASSERTIVENESS can best be illustrated in a short space by another example:

> X and Y were having a conversation:
> X – 'Lets' go out tonight,'
> Y – 'Lovely, Shall we go to the play or the film?'
> X – 'I don't mind' (but meaning 'I want you to want what I want').
> Y – 'I don't mind either' (but meaning 'I know what I want but I don't want to upset you if it's not what you want').
> *Outcome:* Tedious arguing, false giving-way, bad feeling that neither will make a decision, so in the end it gets too late to go out anyway.

But, using assertive answers, the result could be different:

> X – 'There's not a lot between the two, but I would prefer the play because John at work enjoyed it and I'd like to compare notes with him.'
> Y – 'I really wanted to see the film, but I can see it on video anytime, and it's not often we go to a play together.'
> *Outcome*: Each knows the other's position clearly. Each is satisfied, and their mutual agreement makes the outing more enjoyable than either had anticipated.

It is worth looking closely at the way we frame our conversation, at the assumptions and demands which are hidden in the words we choose – or even in the things we choose not to say – because the differences in the response we get can be so great.

ASSERTIVENESS makes use of straightforward statements that are:
non-aggressive;
non-defensive;
non-presumptive; that is, they are not loaded with innuendo about the involvement of the other. What part the other chooses to play is left to him/her to state, it is not presumed.

When making use of assertive techniques the speaker puts

the position from his/her point of view without implicating the other.

Assertiveness aims to avoid any suggestion of 'scoring' over the other, of placing 'guilt' or 'fault' on either side, of playing one-up-manship or putting-the-other-down. If there is any 'fault' to be laid it is fixed, wherever possible, upon circumstances.

Assertiveness has a lot to do with Listening, Allowing, and Accepting.

Perhaps the following story helps to express these ideas in practice:

> The couple had had a disturbed night; the baby had been demanding extra food from Mum. She was touched when Dad rolled over and sleepily said he would get the morning tea. She lay awake enjoying the novelty of having tea brought to her. But he didn't move. 'Ah!' she crowed to herself, 'he's let me down again,' and she felt herself building up all the petty grievances she could use as ammunition to lower him later. She went over in her mind the different ways she could concoct of saying, 'You don't care! you promised' (neither of which, she realized, were strictly true). Oh dear, the whole day would now be spoilt. It would be full of her accusations of his feebleness and his lack of appreciation for her goodness and self-sacrifice. They would probably end the day by not speaking to each other.
> She pulled herself up sharply. Was this the sort of day SHE WANTED?? In the long run was it IN HER INTEREST to carry on in that way? Could SHE CHOOSE to alter it? She decided to discard her whining and try what a direct, objective approach would do.
> Getting out of bed she went through the usual routine of getting the morning tea. As she returned he woke properly and accepted the cup she gave him.
> 'I felt very put out you didn't get the tea after you had offered to. What happened?'
> 'Did I? I must have been talking in my sleep. I wish I had been awake and could have got it for you for a

change.' And he gave her an understanding hug which set the whole day fair after all.

Assertiveness brings freedom from all those endless invidious insinuating innuendoes which we spend so much of our time making up about other people's behaviour. And at the same time all that nervous energy is released to spend in more constructive ways of living. Particularly when we are stressed and feeling hard done by, the spiral of 'poor little me' and 'horrible them' saps our energy and makes every situation worse. Breaking into that spiral may take an effort but it not only lets others off the hook, it makes life so much more enjoyable for me as well.

★　★　★　★　★

All the examples so far have been dealing with degrees of irritation. What about full-blown ANGER? Is choice any use then? It's a bit late to opt for equilibrium and release in the middle of a fully developed rage; but if we look out for the stress-signs which build up to the rage – by recognizing, listening, allowing – there is plenty we can do. We can *choose to re-channel* the anger before it reaches the stage of harming others.

> For a start, I am going to look at what makes me *really* angry. Usually there is an element of me-not-getting-what-I-want. It may be that I am angry on behalf of someone else's mistreatment, but it is still basically because what has happened isn't the way I would have had it happen. So I am angry that my way has been rejected; that I not in control; that I am not after all at the helm. I may feel that I am being told I am not good enough, that I don't belong, and then I feel I must take it out on something over which I do have control – often it is something weaker and even more powerless than me. Something on which I can work out my violent feelings. Something I can spoil, so that I am not the only thing that isn't good enough.

Does any of this ring bells?
What to do, when this is boiling up inside me?

COPING WITH ANGER

What can I do when I am at boiling point?

There is a recipe to bear in mind when I feel I am about to explode:

1. *Recognize the anger.* It is mine, it is part of me, I cannot disassociate myself from it by saying it came from somewhere else. It is up to me to deal with it.

If it is actually at boiling point, there are two choices.

If it is just coming up to the boil, there are three.

2. *Make the choices.* There is little point in waiting for someone else or something else to take the anger from me; this can happen if I am lucky, but I can rely more positively on what is going to happen if I deal with it myself. The choices open to me are these:

When the anger is at boiling point:

(a) Am I going to hurt someone else? Is this the *only* way to be satisfied? or

(b) Can I release this anger on to something *harmlessly?*

For instance, by (suggestions from students)
    bashing saucepan lids
    screaming in the bath
    beating the radiator with a cardboard roll
    digging violently in the garden
    yelling into my pillow
    tearing up the telephone directory
    running for all I am worth – anywhere.

When anger is coming up to the boil, the three-fold choice is to

(a) repress, deny, reject it. This is seldom a good thing, it will come up again somewhere else.

(b) suppress, control, hide it *temporarily*. This is often the immediate expedient, but the suppressed anger will have to be met sometime.

(c) disperse, defuse it and *use* it; that is, channel the emotional energy into physical energy – sport, work excercise, chopping wood, scrubbing the floor, or *creativity*.

3. *Relate it*

The anger will have to be related in two ways:

(a) It must be related to its source. Can anything be done to alter or avoid the stressor which triggered the anger? Can I usefully do anything to adapt to the stressor?

In addition, where possible

(b) the anger and its sources ought to be *related* to an understanding confidant. (Ways and means of doing this have been looked at in chapter 6.)

The more energy that can be diverted from negative

feelings and ideas towards positive ones the better; and the more energy that can be spent on affirming rewards rather than bemoaning hurts (as long as they are not denied) the more life will be enjoyable. The more we can harness the drive in stress to our own purposes, the more it will work for us rather than against us.

Anger, as an emotion or tool to use to get what we want is usually inept. It can sometimes work, but in such a clumsy and inefficient way that as a means of forcing our own way it is thoroughly unreliable.

★   ★   ★   ★   ★

Most negative emotions contain some element of anger. In many negative states the anger is repressed because it is too uncomfortable or too 'anti-social' to acknowledge. We have been conditioned during our up-bringing to look upon all anger as 'bad'. The element of anger that is there can't get out and it turns in upon itself. My anger turned upon myself will make me feel more

depressed	anxious
guilty	resentful
frustrated	suspicious
hurt, aggrieved	jealous

so it is worth taking steps to come to terms with what is inside me.

As we mature we can choose to identify and allow our anger and its sources and then choose what to do with it. A great deal of social anger goes into BLAME, and we are most of us adept at the BLAME GAME.

Carrying around bad feelings can be an intolerable burden. We feel pulled down, deflated, made smaller, by the weight of the burden. We have to either pretend we don't possess bad feelings, or we have to make ways of passing the burden on to something else. Usually it is on to *somebody* else. So we set out to play the Blame Game.

THE BLAME GAME

In the Blame Game there is a winner and a loser.
I, naturally, assume I am the winner.
There are four playing positions:

1st position

I am pure and virtuous. My hands are immaculately clean,
and I take great pains to keep them so.

If anyone throws any doubt upon my virtuousness, I keep
virtuously quiet. I resist hitting back, though perhaps I
might award myself the luxury of a little sullen self-
righteousness. But all the time I am collecting scores,
storing up ammunition, secretly adding to my stock of
credit points.

2nd position

I spy someone else Doing Something Bad.

Because I'm so virtuous I have earned the right to tell
him so. I have kept my hands clean, so I have a special
duty to show him how dirty he has made his. Maybe I
can even allow myself to raise my voice.

3rd position

Suddenly, unexpectedly, out it all comes. I find I am yelling
out all the points I have been secretly piling up and,
like a flame-thrower, my venom burns and sears my
opponent as if he was the only faulty one in the world.

4th position

Instantly I, the virtuous one, am the guilty party! I am the
one who reacted and has turned dark! I am no longer
clean! Has that blaming done anyone any good?

Why is this preposterous game so popular? . . .

Is it because we haven't grown up enough yet to bear the
responsibility of having dirty hands ourselves? If we detect
grime in ourselves do we feel we have to get rid of it on to

someone else? Would it be less harmful if we put it on to *something* else instead? Or at least admitted to *sharing* the stain?

This is where the tactics of assertiveness and channeling anger come in useful. Once we can recognize ourselves projecting our own faults and fears on to other people to their detriment (and, in the long run, our own discomfort), we can use very simple ploys to avoid getting tied up in the Blame Game. Ways of avoiding getting knotted in the Blame Game include:

☐ Things like replacing 'you always', and 'you never' with 'you sometimes'; or 'you promised' with 'we agreed'; and 'you've got to' with 'let's';

☐ Things like putting the blame on to circumstances rather than people; 'You're late!' then becomes 'The traffic must have been heavy'.

☐ Things like asking for help in sorting out a problem rather than blaming someone for creating the problem; 'Who's pinched my hairbrush?' becomes 'Can anyone help me find my hairbrush?'

☐ Things like recognizing 'scapegoating' for what it is – passing over the responsibility; 'It's all your fault' becomes 'It's our fault, let's sort this out together.'

☐ Things like choosing to let the blame stop with me and resisting the urge to pass it on; not letting other people's projections get to me but recognizing that if the cap doesn't fit, there is no point in getting upset.

☐ Things like seeing the situation from the other person's point of view – it will look surprisingly different standing in their shoes.

☐ Things like knowing that anyone can find offence – a fence, or barrier, or obstacle – but it is the clever ones who find a gate.

Any of these and suchlike ploys can be used to defuse negative situations. If they are practised and put to good use, the burden of bad feelings becomes infinitely less.

But it's up to me to choose

★ ★ ★ ★ ★

We spend most of our time, whether we are conscious of it or not, in choosing between alternatives and making minute decisions. If we look after the small decisions, the big ones come more easily.

Making Decisions is a matter of weighing up the advantages and disadvantages of behaving – or thinking or speaking – in certain ways. Choosing can be extraordinarily painful for some people. Sometimes the use of paper and pencil is helpful. Two sheets are needed, one headed with the action to be taken, for instance 'Buying a dog', and the other headed with the opposite, 'Not buying a dog'. Then two columns are made on each sheet headed 'Benefits' (that is, the advantages of having a dog) and 'Costs' (that is, the disadvantages of having a dog).

In each column anything that comes to mind, whether it seems significant or marginal, is listed and put down, in any order.

Points are then allotted to each entry, according to their importance to you within a range of 1–5. Then add the totals, and by comparing their size you will have an instant guide to the way the decision should be taken!

This system can be applied for relatively trivial decisions (shall I walk or take the car?) or for major ones (shall I offer myself to work for the Samaritans?) with just the same usefulness.

AWARENESS EXERCISE

Take a few minutes to go over in your mind any incidents you can remember where you have been angry, or used blame to try to get what you wanted. Did it succeed? Was any situation, in the long run, improved? Did it do you, or anyone else, any lasting good? When did you last point your finger? Did it amuse you, or make you feel good?

Behaviour is seldom right/wrong, but rather it reflects the circumstances and conditioning of the person doing it and the way they have learnt to cope with their own tensions. Circumstances and coping skills can be improved, but seldom by using blame.

The popular media today have a passion for pinning the blame! We are encouraged everyday to take an interest in winning and losing, making heads roll, allocating victory and ensuring that somebody pays for defeat. Are there alternative ways of dealing with difficulties in our personal lives? Giving and taking a little? Negotiating and compromising? Sharing and working together? Which way produces less harmful stress?

This entire chapter is about taking on the responsibility for my own choices. Once I have done that, the stressors I find in my life are less likely to produce destructive stress-signs, because I shall be more in charge. The wholeness I am reaching out for will be nearer.

———CHRISTIAN OUTLOOK———

A chapter dealing with personal choice, anger, and blame obviously cannot conclude without a reference to guilt and judgement. The historical God of the Old Testament was portrayed as a righteous judge who watched from heaven to see that his people kept to the letter of his law – or what they interpreted as his law. Right and Wrong were very clear, and people felt safe in the knowledge that their boundaries were unchangeable. In normal human development all children go through this stage of needing to know what is acceptable to those in authority around them. But the time comes when we have to take the responsibility upon ourselves of discovering what is valid and of good integrity, and what is false and second-hand. We have to shoulder right and wrong and make decisions between black and white or grey personally for ourselves.

At this point the Christian and the non-Christian viewpoints diverge fundamentally. Many people would insist that all they need to gain control over their strong emotions and reach wholeness of body, mind, feeling and spirit is to discover and develop their own personal inner resources to the full. Christians would say that this is not enough, that in order to reach our full wholeness we need to be dependent for strength and guidance on an outside wisdom and power. They would say further, that this outside source of vision and creativity is both available and inexhaustible, and that it comes in love; that the peace and joy and assurance it brings is incomparably greater than that brought by other means, and that the model we are given of it is Jesus Christ.

Christ made choices – strange ones according to his times, and against some of the accepted rules of his day; Christ was angry at times, and he squarely (though rarely) blamed those who misled the people. The question for us here is DOES CHRIST BLAME US? Do we feel his heavy hand upon US? Is it because we feel that we have first been judged and we feel guilty that we are so ready to judge other people? But have we been judged?

Stop here and really consider. It may be a turning point. Are we passing on to others the judgement we *imagine* is bearing down upon us, and that we can't bear?

Christ came in love and compassion and understanding. He gave no judgement that is too heavy to bear; he gave no judgement so heavy that we can have the need to pass it on; we have no judgement to pass on. Indeed he told us to resist judging each other. Our choices and with them our responsibility is totally our own; they cannot be applied to others. We each have our own individual shape, our own individual personal resources. Yet in spite of his own abundant personal resources Jesus Christ was totally dependent on God the Father for strength and wisdom and guidance. He expects us to be too.

I am a dependant of God's . . . I am God's dependant.

There is a very strange thing about the word DEPENDANT (meaning 'hanging from').

Look at it again . . . dependant . . .

Now alter two bits of the first and sixth letters and look at this word . . . repentant . . .

> If I hang on to God, if I acknowledge I am dependent on him for strength, purpose, wholeness growing, I will be like the small child holding on to his father's hand as they cross the busy traffic. I will have three of my four limbs free to do what I like with, but my warmth and security and guidance come from the hand which hangs on to my father. And the child will arrive at the other side whole and safe – except for the bruises I get from wilfully tackling the traffic as I crossed! And these will be treated by my father.

Repentance is acknowledging this dependency, and adding a bit of old fashioned rue for one's wilfulness.

So we have to be responsible for our own choices, our own anger, our own blaming. God will not blame us, but if we let go his hand and deny our dependency we may blame ourselves. And that state of separation and self-blame has been likened to the worst form of wilderness.

We bring this state of wilderness (some call it 'hell') upon ourselves. If we accept that choices belong to us, then that state of separation and self-blame also belongs to us. We may mistake it for the blame of God, but there is no blame from him. It is we who choose.

9
Making space

SPACE is a word that has cropped up frequently,
> The space that is me . . .
> The space to be me . . .

This chapter is about making space not only for the body and the mind, but also for feelings and the spirit. It is quite a tall order. It helps to look at it in this 'wholeness' diagram:

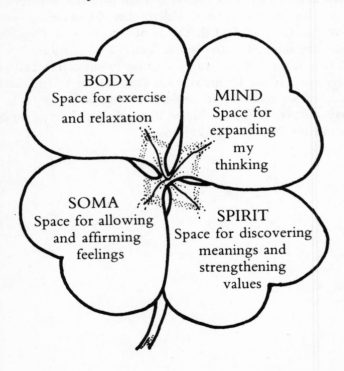

BODY
Space for exercise and relaxation

MIND
Space for expanding my thinking

SOMA
Space for allowing and affirming feelings

SPIRIT
Space for discovering meanings and strengthening values

The space we make can be used for:
- ☐ doing something I really want to do;
- ☐ for just being;
- ☐ for relaxation – both social and deeper relaxation;
- ☐ for meditation of various sorts;
- ☐ but primarily, *for knowing myself.*

In using space, two vital principles apply:
- ☐ The first is that *quantity is not the same as quality;*
- ☐ and the second is that *aloneness is not the same as loneliness.*

To create this sort of space, three things are needed:

PLACE, TIME, and TENACITY.

To illustrate how all this can be put into practice here are some of the ways found by different people:

> One student deliberately created a space for himself by occupying the gents' for 10 mintues each lunchtime at his work. Another found a special tree where he had a bench; he called it his 'peace tree' and others knew that when he was there he was not to be disturbed. One woman cleared the space under the stairs in her house, shielded it with a rope curtain, and placed a low table and chair in it. Her family knew that it was 'her' place, and did their best to leave her quiet when she went there.

All these people knew it needed tenacity to find a place and a time just for themselves, to recover from the demands of life and to 'collect their wits' before tackling the next task.

CREATING A PLACE

☐ It doesn't have to be a large or beautiful place – although where available they both are very desirable – but it does have to be somewhere where I can be uninterrupted. A corner of a room that is wholly mine for books, notes, pictures will mean more to me than a whole large room shared with others.

☐ It doesn't have to be in a building – it can be a particular spot I can go to that has associations of peace and balance and ease. Maybe it will be near home, or it may be somewhere I only visit occasionally.

☐ It doesn't always have to be somewhere where I can be alone – sometimes I may want to share my space with a valued friend, someone with whom I enjoy being quiet.

☐ It doesn't even have to be a physical place – it can be a mental place, a place of stillness that I can imagine when I am on my own at the bus-stop, or going to sleep, or waiting for a delivery or at any un-busy moment. A definite place I can recall at will.

☐ But it *does* have to be a place I have deliberately chosen, and that I have deliberately planned to keep for the purpose of exploring my own space. *And usually it will need considerable tenacity to keep it special.*

MAKING TIME

There are countless ways of making the most of time. To use the phrase 'Sorry, I haven't the time,' is simply a way of saying that other issues have priority at that moment. It is often said that it is the busiest people who can fit something more in; how they do it is through techniques of *time management.*

In the context of this chapter, finding time in which to create a space for me means looking at my weekly timetable, and that of those with whom I live, and devising some period during which minimum demands will be made upon me.

This parcel of 'own' time doesn't have to be of a certain length – it may be ten minutes every other day, a half-day every fortnight, twenty minutes night and morning, or it might be a few days spent away in silence each year. The *quantity* of time is secondary to the fact that it has been set aside deliberately to be spent in the way I most want. It may be that I choose to spend it reading, following a hobby, visiting a friend, or just being on my own, but it is MY space.

It is very important to be aware of the *quality* of time. Twenty minutes of total attention can effect more than two hours of wandering attention. Sometimes a fleeting, but very conscious, moment of time can make all the difference to one's toleration of stress.

> When life seems to be endlessly looking after other people, it is all the more important to relish the minutes spent on one's own. In the bath, washing-up, watering the garden, or even lying awake at night. Each scrap of aloneness can be savoured, can be heightened by awareness of 'quality'.

TEN QUICK TIPS
FOR MAKING BETTER USE OF TIME

1. *Take time to plan.* It is often claimed that using as much as 10 per cent of time in planning will pay off in saving total time.
2. *List everything that has to be done.*
3. *Rank the list in order of necessity.* If this proves difficult, make three categories in which to put the various tasks; things that *must* be done; things it would be *nice* to get done; and things that could be left to another day.
4. *Which of these things could be delegated?* How? To whom? When?
5. *Who could be approached for help or advice?* How? When?
6. *Number the minutes each task will take.* Add up the total, including time for eating and relaxing. Is it less than the 960 minutes we each have to spend every day? Allowing for 8 hours in bed, we still have 16 x 60 minutes every day. Rewrite the list in logical steps for the day.
7. *Use the nooks and crannies of time.* Water the garden, or part of it, before breakfast; telephone while anything automatically timed is going on – such as the microwave

oven, the electronic typewriter or printer, but not while the bacon is frying or the bath is running!

8. *Use shorter sentences* when speaking or writing. Develop a sense of succinct expression. Learn to skim read.

9. *Pace interviews* or conversations with others. Learn to say, 'I've got to . . . in 45 mins/at 2 o'clock/before tea; do you mind, that's when I'll have to leave you'.

10. *Forward plan.* Anything can be accomplished as long as it is planned sufficiently ahead of time. Break up the necessary preparation into small chunks well ahead of the actual date. Write these smaller goals down on appropriate days in the diary.

A short word of warning: in getting rid of some of the feelings of disorder in our lives, it can be only too easy to squeeze out feelings of kindliness, gentleness, laughter, delight. Others may not *need* such control in their lives: the order I need may not be in order for others. It is not my place to presume that it is; it is my place to allow others to live their lives their way, not mine.

★   ★   ★   ★   ★

A way of being at ease with time, making it flow, and adding to its quality, is to become more aware of the spaces *within the body*. Think of all the channels through which the systems of the body function, or flow. Blood vessels, air passages, food pipes, even the channels of excretion: when waiting, or listening, or watching, or resting, or just sitting-in-between-times, do I take up positions which block, and obstruct, and 'stress' these channels? Just out of habit? Such as the left-hand one in Figure 6? Or do I take the opportunity to deliberately keep the channels open and 'flowing'? It is no coincidence that the classic position of stress constricts *all* our body systems, while the relaxed position frees them.

If my physical systems flow freely, it is remarkable how this will be reflected in my thoughts and emotions – they are more likely to flow freely too. The Chinese speak of the importance of *'chi'*, that is the life-force or energy, flowing unobstructed through our being, allowing us to be freely creative. Many of the complementary therapies such as acupuncture and reflexology are based on these opposite positions: the body being stressed with channels obstructed, or relaxed and open with channels flowing.

Figure 6. **'Blocked' and 'Open' Positions**

Typical stressed position
On edge of support
Head down
Eyes averted
Neck dragging
Shoulders up and hunched
Back stiff
Elbows in
Arms self-protective
Hands clenched, closed
Tummy tight
Hips turned in
Knees crossed tightly
Legs knotted
Toes turned up

Withdrawn inwards: body channels of circulation, digestion, respiration, excretion are constricted and choked.

Typical open position
Well back in seat, trusting support
Head up and balanced
Eyes making contact
Straight neck, weight balanced
Shoulders down, connecting not
    carrying
Back long and relaxed
Elbows and arms loose
Hands open, receptive
Tummy soft and easy
Hips turned out
Knees at ease
Legs separated
Feet and toes down, well supported

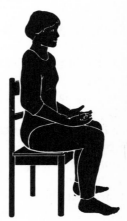

Outward-looking, accepting: channels are unblocked and open.
LIFE IS FLOWING.

So, if I take control of the position of my body, I can 'free-up' my living. My body, mind, emotions and spirit are 'freed' by the simple decision to take charge of my body position. My use of time will take on a freer, more open quality, and my sense of space and my place within it will be more open, more relaxed.

TENACITY

Tenacity means *'holding together'*. It's a matter of being persistent in finding space and sticking with it when it's there, not being too easily swayed or distracted. And this applies whatever use is being made of the space available, whether it is with a hobby, practising deep relaxation, meditating, or simply being.

This sort of tenacity is particularly needed when I find I am alone. It may be that I am physically on my own, or that I am alone in silence. If I stick with it, I will discover that to be alone isn't necessarily to be lonely. Tenacity is to do with *concentration* – a word meaning *'bringing to a common centre, con-centre'* – and that exactly describes what happens when we concentrate. The way in which odd thoughts and concerns can deflect our intentions and distract our thoughts is a worry to many people. These wafting ideas should be neither fought nor denied; if they are allowed just to float easily into *and equally easily out of* our minds, rather like inconsequential bubbles, the main theme we really want to hold on to will stay. The ripples stirred by the pebble will flow *out* while the central idea remains.

People under heavy stress find the ideas of determination and concentration particularly difficult. But letting go may be the one most important thing they need to do. Perhaps those around them can be persuaded to help in supporting the patch of quiet they find; perhaps it will just need the courage to ask for such co-operation.

The understanding father of one family with three young

children willingly read a story to them before breakfast while his wife practised deep relaxation because he realized the stress she was under. In return she kept them quiet in the evening while he watched his favourite TV programme. The whole family benefited.

So having found some time, and a place, and having decided to stick with it, let's turn to DEEP RELAXATION.

DEEP RELAXATION

Why DEEP relaxation? Isn't *any* relaxation good enough?

The word 'to relax' means to loosen, to relieve, to release. That is, to make less tight, less strict, less rigorous, and to set free.

In everyday use relaxation happens in many ways; having a good laugh, going to the pictures, letting your hair down at a party, enjoying exercise, or slouching in a 'comfy' chair in front of the TV. So far, so good. But in all these activities muscles are either actively being used, or they are in a state of readiness to be used. They retain some 'tone'. In none of them are they 'released' or 'set free'.

Our muscle fibres are unusual in that they are fully at rest when they are long. When they are at work they contract and are short and thick.

The three basic positions for each muscle in our bodies are:

LONG	REGULAR	SHORT
released and relaxed	toned and waiting	tensed and working

Most of us, most of the time, react to the constant stressors in today's world by remaining in the middle position. We are in a habitual state of physical readiness to respond to alarm. Because the energy that is prepared cannot be immediately released it is locked up in our tight muscles. Not only when we are consciously alert, but when resting or asleep our muscles remain toned. Nervous and very active people may have a chronic position of muscle shortening, spasm, for hours or even days at a time. Those who live with high levels of stress in their lives find it difficult to release their muscles totally even when the stress is positive and enjoyable.

It is not only relief to exhausted and aching muscles that deep relaxation brings, it has other researched benefits too:

☐ It has been said that ten minutes deep relaxation frees more energy than hours 'resting' in a bad position in a chair.

☐ Deep relaxation affects our over-active minds too; having something positive to concentrate on, like the technique of identifying muscle-groups and controlling them, brings calm and a sense of purpose.

☐ Deep relaxation affects an over-active imagination by quietening it.

☐ Deep relaxation lowers blood pressure, relieves the circulation, reduces pulse rate, slows breathing.

☐ Deep relaxation even reaches those muscles not under voluntary control, such as the heart and the stomach, enabling them to relax and rebalance their functions.

☐ Deep relaxation calms an irritable bowel and an over-sensitive bladder.

☐ Other medical relief has been received from eczema, asthma, insomnia, headaches, dysmenorrhoea . . . to name but a few common conditions.

☐ Deep relaxation may lead into meditation. In Eastern cultures exotic claims are made for the state of detachment from pain, sorrow, fear, lust and covetousness which is reached by those who practise deep meditation regularly.

There are many millions of people living in the West who claim a greater balance and freedom and enjoyment in their lives as a result of regularly using deep meditation.

☐ Since deep relaxation makes us become more tolerant and accepting of ourselves, it strengthens tolerance and acceptance in our family relationships, and thereby they too become enriched.

☐ Anybody can do it!

Just in case any reader is still in doubt about the everyday effectiveness of deep relaxation on everyday people, this is a piece of everyday experience:

> With a certain amount of inner trepidation, a teacher suggested to a group of lively 16 and 17-year-old students that they might like to try some deep relaxation. Agreement was unanimous, and most of the boys and girls asked if they could stretch out on the floor.
>
> At the start of the silence, the teacher was conscious of hazards such as giggling, someone who complained of a bad neck, sniffing from a hay-fever sufferer, someone complaining of pins and needles, a loose (and rampant?) wasp, a builder bull-dozing immediately outside the window. 'Shame', she thought, 'not much chance of relaxation here.'
>
> Ten lovely silent minutes later the group slowly roused itself. The bad neck, sniffing, the pins and needles had disappeared; no one claimed to have noticed the bull-dozer; giggling had ceased, and even the wasp had settled comfortably quiet on a curtain. Best of all was 'Can we do that again next time please?'

HOW TO SET ABOUT DEEP RELAXATION

Over the last decades there have been so many advocates of different techniques of deep relaxation that newcomers can understandably feel confused. Different methods appeal to different personalities and circumstances, but it is not the method that is important so much as the effect achieved.

The aim here is to convince readers that deep relaxation is worth trying, and to offer some of the various ideas that have been around and are well-tested.

The run-up to deep relaxation:
For those who are fit, some would recommend strong exercise before settling down to relax (many athletes would relax before exercising!).

For those with aching muscles, the preference would be for 'easing' movements, designed to release spasm but not to over-work the muscles.

For those with minimal time to spare, some teachers recommend that a quick 'flex and flop' is better than nothing – an example of this is given below.

For those who are aware of muscle 'knots', local pressure put directly over the tender spot with fingers or thumb and kept there for a few seconds can help to release the tension. Relaxation then becomes easier.

For those who appreciate mental preparation, there are images which can be helpful. The car that is in overdrive and needs to be braked in order to avoid burn-out has been helpful to many, and the image of *'Let-up'* rather than *'Laid-up'* has convinced even workaholics.

For some, the techniques of deep breathing are an important element of deep relaxation; others are aware of the difficulties that attach to over-conscious breathing. It will become deep and regular eventually anyway.

POSITIONING

Most people agree that comfort is important for deep relaxation, though some prefer that muscles should be 'pulled out', as it were, by extended positioning. So, some teachers supply myriads of pillows for support, while others recommend straight limbs on a hard floor. Followers of Yoga make use of a sustained stretch in some muscles even while they are relaxing.

Many people choose simply to sit. If possible this should be in a supportive chair, with the spine straight and upright (the vertebrae of the spinal column will in fact support themselves if they are allowed to be in a position of balance, and no back rest will be necessary). The bottom should be placed well into the base of the chair-back so that full use is made of the seat of the chair. Thighs should be at right angles (or less) to the trunk. The knees should not be crossed but be left loose and unconstricted – it makes it easier for them to be held like this if the heels are turned slightly outwards on the floor. Feet should be flat on the floor in touch with the ground. Hands may be resting quietly in the lap, open and receptive rather than closed or clasped. The head should be held upright and not allowed to drop forwards or sideways or with the chin too raised – any variance from the point of perfect balance on the neck causes strain. See Figure 6.

Be aware of where the body is being supported, whether you are lying on a bed or the floor or sitting or kneeling on a relaxation stool. Where are the pressure points? How is the weight of the body being taken into the ground? Can you trust the support enough to give up your weight to it?

A little knowledge of physiology can help as you imagine how your muscles work. One set of muscles achieves *one* movement. In order to achieve the *opposite* movement another set of muscles comes into play. Look at your thumb, as you hold this book. Move it across towards the centre of the page (or the centre of your hand); now let go that movement and notice where the thumb rests. Next move your thumb away from the centre as far as it will reach – then let go. Notice the difference in the two 'let go' positions.

Here is a quick try-out of what will happen to muscles that are deeply relaxed:

Clench your fist tightly, feel its iron tightness; let go. Look at the position of the fingers. Now stretch your fingers outwards (using the opposite muscles to the clench); feel the length and pull in your finger-tips . . . let go. Look at the position of your fingers – how is it different to the other 'let go'? Which is the most relaxed?

Now hunch your shoulders up near your ears, feel the tightness in your muscles; let go. Notice their position. Now pull your shoulders down towards your fingers as far as they will go; feel the pull . . . let go. Notice the position of your shoulders now – how is it different to the previous 'let go'. Which is the most relaxed?

Lastly frown as hard as you can, feel the skin being squeezed between your brows . . . let go? Now raise your eyebrows as far as they will go; feel the skin going up into your hairline . . . let go. Notice the position of your forehead now – how is it different to the previous 'let go'? Which is the most relaxed?

You have been doing reciprocal movements, counterbalancing some of the typical positions of stress. It is difficult to command a stressed muscle to relax, but when you feel a particular tightness you can learn to do the opposite movement which will 'pull out' the stress and relieve it. Use the idea of introducing 'space' between muscles, and between muscle fibres.

THE TECHNIQUES

☐ Perhaps the most familiar technique is that of progressive tensing and relaxing of the muscles in the body, starting with the toes and gradually working up towards the head.

☐ Other techniques use a similar series, deliberately detensing the muscles, but thinking of larger groups at a time, and starting from the head going downwards to the toes.

☐ Some techniques don't 'tense' at all, but simply encourage relaxation by using imagery – massage, a rolling heaviness, serene music, warmth, softness, spreading space, abandonment.

☐ There are other methods to do with high technology which can help in deep relaxation; the use of computers for scanning 'nervous' activity, hormone production, and in particular instruments for bio-feedback. Most of this equipment is operated by professionals, although smaller machines for personal bio-feedback are now on the market. These can be very helpful in gauging the rate at which relaxation is being self-regulated.

☐ Most techniques advise a beginner to make use of a taped 'talk-down' or, better still, start with a group. Some people have found it helpful to gather a few like-minded friends together in one of their homes, enlist the help of a teacher for a few sessions, and then continue on their own.

☐ It is helpful to bear in mind, especially when doing a DIY relaxation, the key words – warm, soft, heavy, spreading, let go.

There are very many different *practices* of relaxation on offer; the really important thing is for each person to find the method that suits them. Some people respond to an authoritarian package of 'do it this way because it works', and others prefer something that they have personally adapted to suit themselves.

There are also differences of *principle*; it depends whether people prefer:

☐ to learn the sensation of joints and muscles that are in tension, as it were with full power switched on, and then compare this with the sensation of joints and muscles that are at rest, having switched the power off; or

☐ to use the imagination to melt any tension that is already there. (Some find it quite difficult to switch off the power completely once it has deliberately been switched on.)

The difference is between *doing and stopping*, and *using imagination*. Both types of exercise bring release from physical tension.

EXAMPLES OF TWO TYPES OF RELAXATION METHODS

Physical release using the muscles

This is done as a regular series of muscle actions. Each is held for about five seconds; if it is held for too long cramp might develop. When you let it go, do so quickly, all at once and not too gently or slowly, so you can get to know the contrasting sensation. The exercise may be done in a chair or lying down on the floor or the bed, whichever suits you best. There is a definite sequence of actions, but once these are learnt the relaxation can be practised anywhere and at anytime.

1. If possible, have your shoes off; press the ball of your feet down and spread your toes wide. Hold them there for a few seconds, then let go.

Take time to feel the difference between the two positions . . . Do it again until the sensation of release becomes familiar and you can enjoy it . . .

2. Tense your calf muscles and lift your knee-caps; hold them tightly for a few seconds, then let go.

Take time to feel the difference . . . Do it again until the sensation of release becomes familiar and you can enjoy it.

3. Squeeze your bottom, upper thighs, pelvic floor; hold them hard, as if to lift them off the seat or floor (but don't in fact!), then let go.

Take time to feel the difference . . . Do it again until the sensation of release becomes familiar and you can enjoy it.

4. Flatten your tummy against your spine, breathe out (raising your diaphragm), and let go. Your abdomen is now soft and easy.

Take time to feel the difference . . . Do it again until the sensation of release becomes familiar and you can enjoy it.

5. Tighten the muscles you know around the top of your chest, inner shoulders, hold them tight; then let go. Breathe in and out, easily and gently.

Take time to feel the difference . . . Do it again until the sensation of release becomes familiar and you can enjoy it.

6. Tense your arms, clench your fists, hold them hard; then let go. Feel the spread, the openness of your relaxed arms and fingers. Do it again, paying special attention to your hands, spread them wide open, stretching the fingers while your arm is hard. Let go.

Take time to feel the difference . . . Do it again until the sensation of release becomes familiar and you can enjoy it.

7. Tense your neck, either by pressing the back of your head into the floor if you are lying, or making the tendons stand out if you are sitting. Hold it there for a few seconds, then let go.

Take time to feel the difference . . . Do it again until the sensation of release becomes familiar and you can enjoy it.

8. Clench your jaw, clamping your teeth together. Don't grind them, just hold them hard. Let go. Notice your lips will stay together – just touching – but your tongue will rest in your lower jaw, leaving a space between it and the roof of your mouth. You will feel more space, more openness at the back of your mouth.

Take time to feel the difference . . . Do it again until the sensation of release becomes familiar and you can enjoy it.

9. Squeeze your eye brows into your hairline – those who can should draw their scalp muscles down; and let go. Think of each of the hairs of your eyebrows and those on your head resting peacefully.

Take time to feel the difference . . . Do it again until the sensation of release becomes familiar and you can enjoy it.

Check that all your body from tip to toe is resting peacefully, totally relaxed and totally switched off. Stay there, enjoying the ease and deep relaxation. Be aware of all the channels in your body being unobstructed, all the energy in it flowing freely.

Physical and emotional release using the imagination

This type of relaxation is about recognizing my support, so that I can give up my weight – physical heaviness, emotional burdens, mental problems – to it, while I take a rest from them.

Firstly, settle into a balanced position, preferably on a high-backed chair. Press your chin in and head back, shruggle your shoulders, draw a circle in the air with your elbows, so that all those muscles take up a position of co-ordinated balance, supporting each other, without uneven strains on any of them.

1. Imagine the weight of your head as a ball. Think of it in a position of perfect balance, resting in the little cusp (or 'egg-cup') at the top of your spine. It can remain there indefinitely, completely poised, giving up all the weight and the cares it carries into the spine which supports it. Let the weight flow out of your head and into your spine. Let the weight of your eyelids, cheeks, lips, jaw, all melt down, carried by your chin into your neck and down your spine. Let it all drop down loosely. Your neck is a carrier. The weight it carries passes right down your spine into your chair – or via your spine into the floor you are lying on.

2. Your shoulders are connected to your spine; drop them down, letting their weight go into your arms. Imagine a wave of warmth spreading from your shoulders downwards, melting all heaviness downward, melting all knots of tension as it goes . . . loosening tightness . . . melting heaviness. This wave of rolling warmth moves slowly down your upper trunk, your chest, your upper arms, melting and warming, loosening the heaviness which drops downwards.

3. The warmth and heaviness flows through your lower trunk, your back and your lower arms into your lap. Your tummy softens, your fingers loosen, and the melted heaviness passes right into your seat. Let it go, all the knots and the cares and the burdens are loosened, flowing down, dropping away.

4. Your bottom is soft and spreading, it gives up all the gathering heaviness into the chair; feel the seat of your chair as it supports you, or the floor supporting you. Feel its strength, its reliability, its steadfast support. Give all your heaviness and weight into it. Your body is limp and warm and soft and relaxed.

5. Now this spreading warmth rolls down into your thighs, melting their tension as it goes, releasing the knots of tightness. Feel them loosen and relax in this rolling warmth. Their weight melts and rolls down your lower legs, the relaxation is irresistible; the warmth softens the tension in your knees and calves which give up the weight that has been flowing down them, into your ankles and feet.

6. And your feet rest on the floor. All the rolling heaviness drops straight down into the floor. Give it all up; the floor can take it. Pass it all over into the ground

The floor, the earth, the ground take it all. Give it all up, all the tightness, all the hardness and all the weight that has loosened. up and melted and passed into the ground. You can remain loose and limp and relaxed and centred in *the gound of your being.* Your are supported, held, nurtured, by the ground, whether you think of that ground as the earth, or your own inner centre, or God; you can – for the moment – give all your weight up while you remain supported strongly, safely, securely, steadfastly.

Stay with that support and stillness for several minutes or as long as you can, comfortably. When you are ready, you can come back knowing that that strength and support is always there, always reliable, always available. Bring some of it with you, draw it up through your feet as you wriggle them, through your legs as you move them, and into your body as you prepare to get up. Draw on that strength and support and take it into your daily life.

BE CAREFUL. It may take beginners by surprise how complete the deep relaxation can be; care must always be taken to 'come out' of it slowly and gently. If your eyes have been closed, open them quietly; wriggle the fingers and toes to re-alert the circulation, take a few moments to prepare to get up, don't bounce up. If you have been lying down bend your knees and roll over on to your side before attempting to lift yourself up. It will take your systems quite a little while to gather their energies together if they have been deeply relaxed, so give them a chance!

Once one has become reasonably familiar with relaxation it can be used at any time at will. As soon as one feels muscles tighten, tension rise, even unreasonable temper grow, the methods of detensing oneself can be brought into play. For instance, when feeling frustrated at traffic lights, waiting for an important interview, before any sort of performance, when members of the family are late home . . . What other occasions come to your mind? You will become more habitually at ease in stressed situations the more you can call upon deep relaxation at will.

AWARENESS EXERCISE

This is the example of the 'flex and flop' referred to above. It can be practised anywhere, any time, as long as there is a seat with sufficient space around it.

Sit down and *read what you are about to do before you do it.*
Take ONE deep breath,
All at once, and altogether:
    screw up your face, your eyes, nose, mouth, forehead;
    hunch your shoulders as high as you can;
    throw your arms out as far as they will go;
    tighten your abdominal and pelvic muscles as hard as you can;
    stretch your legs out off the floor;
    hold your heels as far away as they will go, but also
    bring your toes up towards your knees;
    Tense everything. Hold it for three seconds . . .

    And flop!!

Breathe out, and stay leaning over your opened knees
    for half a minute . . .
Feel that lovely rushing release . . .

This is an exaggeration of all the classic stressed positions
in one; *don't do it unless you are reasonably fit*; it can be a very
useful 'first aid' for stress if it suits you. But watch yourself,
and only do it if it does help.

———CHRISTIAN OUTLOOK———

Jesus Christ could surely be said to have had more cause for
'busy-ness' than anyone else who has ever lived:

he came with a charge to heal (or 'make whole') the entire
world –
    he had more to get done than any doctor has ever had;

he came with a charge to turn the whole world to a new
way of thinking –
    he had more to get done than any teacher has ever had;

he came to set in motion a world revolution –
    *he had more to get done than any preacher or politician has
    ever had;*

he came with love and comfort and strength for every
sufferer –
    he had more to get done than any social worker has ever had;

And yet he found time to take time out! To make space!

Although the pressure on time was less great in Galilee than
in our Western culture, and although Jesus could well have
felt satisfied with the dollops of time already given to
religious practices in his day, he still made it a priority to
get away to be on his own. He found the time (often at
night) and the place (a lonely place apart) where he could
get away from all the demands made upon him and where
he could make some space for himself.

He inherited a tradition from Isaiah:
'their strength is to sit still . . .'
'in returning and rest shall ye be saved . . .'
'in quietness and confidence shall be your strength . . .'
and from the Psalms:
'commune with thy heart and be still . . .'
'be still and know that I am God . . .'
'return to thy rest O my soul . . .'

But Christ did not only use this sort of space himself. He taught others to use it also:

Luke says, 'Jesus would always go off to some place where he could be alone' (Luke 5:16 JB); and
'when daylight came he left the house and made his way to a lonely place' (Luke 4:42 JB);
but Mark also records that Jesus said to the disciples,
'Come away to some lonely place all by yourselves and rest for a while' . . . and 'So they went off in a boat to a lonely place where they could be by themselves' (Mark 6:31,32 JB).

If Christ, with so much claim upon his time, could make time and find a place for himself, and encouraged others to do so, can't we?

Note

A taped talk-down which helps relaxation has been produced by Wanda Nash for any reader who responds to this chapter. Please send a strong stamped and self-addressed envelope, together with £2.20 to cover costs, to Wanda E. Nash, P.O. Box 159, Basingstoke, Hants, RG21 2QE. Your order will be receipted and returned promptly.

10
Affirmation

This is the last of the groups of stress-skills that are being presented in Part Two, and it deals with the sources of personal strength from which we can be affirmed, or empowered. The final word in the formula for stress-skills is REFLECT, and whereas previous pages have looked at things to do with the mind and the soma, in this chapter we will be reflecting on how to tap the strength of the body and the spirit.

Some people reflect quite happily on their own, and gain their own strength without any external support. However research has shown that most of us – and most particularly when we are under stress – will gain more from what we are doing and will find less harm in the tension of it if we belong to a strong support group. So the emphasis here will be on the value of *groups*.

> There is an old story about a single stick which on its own had difficulty in not breaking under the weight it had to bear; but it got together with others and as soon as a bundle had been made it became impossible to break. Tearing a single sheet of paper is easy, but try tearing it when it has been folded seven times.

Almost everybody has some sort of group support; sometimes it is of their own direct choosing, and sometimes it is just where they happen to find themselves. The *family* is of course the universal basic 'group'; but other groups such as work colleagues, friends who have known us since childhood, neighbours, and the like-minded people we choose as company, can provide support that is equally important. These days the family itself comes in all shapes and sizes, it is no longer true that the average family consists of a father + a mother + two children + a pet. The family group can be a source of enormous and bewildering stress, but equally, when the family meets stress and its causes with a mutual concern and understanding, it can be the source of continuing growth and constant recharging.

Concern, continuing, constant are good group words, so is confirm. They all start with 'con' – meaning 'with'.

★　★　★　★　★

We are all born into a family, and that is the grouping within which most of us first learn how to treat our bodies. For about fifteen years we take on the habits and patterns of those around us. Increasingly we are being encouraged as individuals to judge for ourselves what to put into our bodies, how to listen to the messages they give us, and how to make the most use of the bodily strength that is our only tool. So what about *strengthening the body* against the harms of stress?

Once again, it has been shown time and again that those who look after their bodies well are less harmed by stress, and are better equipped to enjoy its stimulating effects, than those who distance themselves from the details of daily care. It is neither vain nor selfish to keep our bodies in prime condition – as we do even to our cars. It is a proper responsibility.

The main headings to look at in this area are

health-care and well-being,
food, drink and stimulants,
exercise, rest and recreation
and, later, in-filling with deep relaxation and meditation.

LOOKING AFTER MYSELF

Health

My wellness is primarily my own responsibility. If I have symptoms of disease it is proper that I should seek trained advice, but my wellness starts with me – not with my doctor or my spouse or my works company. It is up to me to make sure I use all the help and information that is available, but fundamentally it is I who am in charge of what I eat and drink and do, and that is where wellness begins.

There is today an enormous amount of advice being made available concerning good health; sometimes the difficulty is finding the balance between responsibility and hypochondria or eccentricity. To a large extent I can experiment with ideas and potions without infringing on others, but when a particular enthusiasm produces stress-signs – in myself or others! – it is a good idea to look again at its purpose.

All the early signs of stress discussed in Part One which are to do with my behaviour should be controllable by me as long as I recognize them before they become entrenched. With practice, I should be able to affect most of the physiological stress signs as well. Some of them I can control directly, such as deliberately breathing more slowly and calmly, and some of them I will be able to affect indirectly – such as eating a more balanced diet or practising relaxation. If I can become aware of the times when I am at my lowest – which is also when I am the least tolerant of stress, the most likely to have accidents, and the most open to infection – I can then take steps to lessen the hazards. Recognizing my own particular stressors is a large part of this process.

Health groups are becoming increasingly popular. There are many self-help groups for those with particular health problems (and lists of these are available through a Health Centre, Citizens' Advice Bureau, or local library), but the formation of Well Woman Clubs is answering a need too. Those who feel stressed about their health care, or who feel alone in it, are strongly advised to contact one of these organizations.

Food

Bookshops and news-stands are full of tempting recipes side by side with dietary advice. Most of the principles are by now common knowledge. In order to get the most out of our health we should: avoid regular over-eating; cut down on fat and sugar; eat more fresh fruit and raw vegetables; add fibre and subtract salt. Where possible we should keep away from processed food and be aware of those things to which we are particularly allergic. Most food shops now have taken the labelling of their foodstuffs seriously, so it is easier to know what it is made up of; however we may have to remember to take our spectacles when we go shopping!

Some simple principles are sometimes overlooked:

1. Enjoy what you *do* eat more than missing what you *don't* eat. Savour it, take time over it, swallow it slowly, be the last to finish!

2. If you want to weigh less, just eat less! Develop a tolerance of the feeling of hunger; it is a familiar sensation to most of the world. Eat again only when you are hungry, not out of habit.

3. If you want to be kind to an overworked stomach, imagine all the processing it has to do to your food; then you will be less keen to overload it.

4. Watch those 'snacks'. Calorie-dense tit-bits such as cheese, chocolate, nuts, crisps *are not snacks*: they are main meal foods. 'SNACKS' are fruit, fingers of carrots, celery, cabbage-heart which can be prepared and left in the fridge, toasted stale bread, cream crackers, or even half a cold potato, but *not* foods rich in protein, fat, or sugar. Jelly made with unsweetened fruit juice, and ice cubes made from left-over wine also make good snacks. If you feel empty an hour before a meal, it's better to satisfy it with a hot drink rather than with extra food.

The preparation, offering and receiving of food has subtle

and complex undercurrents that are not always fully taken into account. The relationships around a family meal table are as complicated as a spider's web and can as easily break down. Toddlers and teenagers and older people test and protest, often calling for a great deal of tolerance and acceptance. But there is nothing quite so satisfying and worth working for than the sharing and supporting that can take place at meal-times.

Food groups include cookery clubs, consumer groups, and weight-watching organizations of various sorts. Sharing in the enjoyment of food rather than the fads of food will also reduce any stress that happens to be connected with it.

Drink

The most popular drinks are those with stimulants – tea, coffee, alcohol. Fortunately, the choice of drinks that are primarily thirst-quenching increases in variety every day. In addition to highly advertized commercial drinks, there are mineral waters, fruit juices and cordials of every description, herb teas prepared in England as well those from abroad, milk and its derivatives, and different types of extract such as Bovril, Oxo, Marmite or Yeastrel. Those who want to drink because they are thirsty rather than because they want to be stimulated can have no lack of variety.

Drink consumed in groups is often of the stimulating sort. If it is alcoholic, this can become a stressing difficulty, particularly where driving is concerned.

> Many young people agree in advance who will be giving lifts to whom when the party is over; such a degree of common sense should be taken note of by their elders.

Drink and stimulants

Caffeine is even more socially acceptable than alcohol, and yet it has wide-spread effects. Tannin, caffeine, alcohol and nicotine are all taken on account of the 'lift' they give; yet soon after their consumption the 'lift' reverses, and a further dose is needed to maintain the level.

Try doing without one of these four for a day or two

and watch the result. Unless there are withdrawal symptoms that are too significant, there will be a greater sense of control, a greater calm, and a stronger awareness of being able to cope than had been realized had been previously sacrificed.

All these four stimulants are addictive, but other stimulants may be more socially disruptive. The readers of a book such as this will already be aware of the dangers of artificial stimulants: all of them promise a degree of stress-relief, but experience proves this is totally false.

> Groups are invaluable in helping people who want to get free of the need to rely on stimulants. It can be a long and very difficult business; the more they commit themselves to group working, the more likely they are to succeed.

Exercise
The relationship between exercise and stress is extremely important.
1. The straight follow-on for someone feeling aggressive and angry is to let all that energy loose on sport – preferably competitive sport. But
2. Competition, and particularly violent competition, is extremely stress-full; so only those who can enjoy high stress-levels should choose this line. Those who *think* they enjoy high stress, but in practice cannot tolerate the risk of failure and frustration that goes with it, should keep well away.
3. On the other hand, social exercise that carries with it a lower level of competition satisfies three needs: it releases pent-up energy, it builds up muscle-tone, and it strengthens social support.
4. For many people, the fact that they can no longer physically take part in active exercise is itself a source of stress. There are four options open to them. They can
    (a) do nothing; or they can
    (b) release their energy by watching and barracking others who exercise, perhaps on television;

(c) practise 'easing' movements rather than 'strengthening' movements (these pull out their shortened muscle by counteractive flexion, rather than strain them with exercises designed for body-building);

(d) learn to use isometric exercise: this means strongly tensing and then relaxing different groups of muscles without any obvious action. Such exercises can be practised while sitting or lying or standing, wherever one is: just drawing together the fibres in a group of muscles as strongly as possible and then letting go. The strengthening and releasing effect will both surprise and delight.

The popularity of jogging as an exercise has lessened recently because of the injuries that overtake some enthusiasts. Walking seems to be freer from misuse, and *striding* gives a marvellous sense of purpose and competence. If isometric tensing is used while striding, it can provide enough exercise and exhilaration to suit most people. The whole body can be stretched without an onlooker being aware of anything unusual. Perhaps arm swinging in a public place would be a bit too ostentatious, but a full work-out of

neck turning
pectoral hunching and dropping
shoulder circling
arm rotating
stomach tightening
pelvic tilting
thigh tensing
knee back-pressing
leg rotating
foot raising
toe curling . . . can be carried out unbeknownst to any.

Above all, exercise should be *enjoyed*; various types of music and movement and/or dancing combine delight and muscle-strengthening with relief of stress. For those who are less active, kite-flying brings with it a wonderful sense of space and release. Learning how to juggle, even just in your own room and using bean bags, can also add a feeling of capable control to one's self-worth.

Exercise groups have many functions, many of which relieve stress and strengthen self-esteem. Some team groups also encourage the practise of deep relaxation. The experience of working together at a particular goal always builds up group support, and the feeling that each person is contributing something to the common aim is a great antidote to stress. But if the pressure is on to 'produce the goods' and to reach for a goal that is part of someone else's idea of excellence, care will have to taken that stress does not become an end in itself.

Rest and recreation

As long as any of the above groups are found to be enjoyable and strengthening, they will be recreative. Sometimes just sitting still and actually doing nothing other than 'being' is also recreative. It is not necessary to be 'doing' all the time.

There are occasions when we feel we 'should' be merrier and happier, but we aren't and can't; this is a familiar experience, particularly at the beginning of a holiday.

> On the one hand I will need time to adjust to a different environment and a different pace of living; but on the other, it is sometimes exactly at that moment when pressures are let up, and I don't *have* to continue keeping going, that systems beyond my control take over and depression or illness catches up with me. All I have to do is allow the negative phase to work its way through with as little fuss as possible, realizing that it *is* only a phase, and will pass, Adding disappointment and remorse or self-blame to the situation will only worsen it and make it last longer. If others around me can be helped to understand what is going on and be encouraged to go out and enjoy their own thing, this will be a help too.

Recreation groups are so numerous it is impossible to include them all. As far as the relief of harmful stress and the strengthening of social support is concerned, the same principles apply as have been stated before. Christians and members of religious or ethical groups have an added advantage in that house groups are part of the order of their lives and, given a little encouragement, they are relatively easy to set up. Non-sectarian groups include those who gather regularly for anything – having lunch together, reading poetry, learning lace-making, whatever answers the interests of those who attend.

Difficulties may come when it becomes appropriate for a particular group to cease. Discussion of the particular skills of 'letting go' is included in chapter 22.

★　★　★　★　★

And now we come to what is undoubtedly the most powerful stress-balancer of all: the presence of *focused stillness* in our everyday lives. It has many names, and is used by many people using many different forms:

> among children, we usually call it *day-dreaming*;
>
> among young people, we call it *wonder* – or being in love, or losing oneself;
>
> among adults, it is usually called *meditation* or *contemplation*.

It is use of silence for keeping still, alert, relaxed, and concentrated. Its effect is to *con-centre* ourselves, to affirm our interior strength, and it puts everything else into proportion. Many people *need* it, as an intake from another dimension, as much as a porpoise needs to come up for air. The porpoise is wonderfully adapted to living in a watery world but he is built to survive on air; so we live among material things but we need to quaff now and again from things of the spirit.

MEDITATION AND CONTEMPLATION

The following is a brief description of a subject that has absorbed people for at least thirty centuries. The earliest

recorded evidence of the deliberate practice of concentrated stillness is from Persia, eight centuries before Christ.

This discussion will take the form of four questions:

☐ Why should I be interested in meditation; where does it take me?

☐ What does it claim to bring me?

☐ Who has tried and verified it?

☐ How is it done?

Where does it take me?

On the mundane, physical level, the practice of concentrated stillness following deep relaxation leads one to a state that is the exact opposite to the state of stress; pulse, blood pressure, and breathing rates all go down, the pattern of electrical waves in the brain calms down, resistance to disease goes up and coping responses to alarm and anxiety are strengthened.

On a deeper level, the practice of focused stillness takes me towards my centre, towards wholeness; it fills up the 'dents' and gaps in the area of my spirit; it rebalances my over-active mind, it counteracts my over-active body, it settles my over-active emotions; best of all it feeds my under-nourished and under-active spirit.

> For centuries the Western world has spent its energies on activity and acquisition: to do well means getting more money, more success; in the East to 'do well' is more often a matter of becoming more aware of one's inner spirit, of being still and whole. In the East 'whole' is naturally synonymous with 'holy'. Where are our 'holy men' of the West?

What does it claim to bring?
The language used by practitioners is, they say, only a poor reflection of what it is they are trying to describe. Creative awakening, heightened awareness, imperturbability, mind-fulness of the here and now which carries neither remorse for the past nor phantasy of the future, a life that is flowing not fraughting, a felt knowledge of order in spite of apparent chaos, peace and warmth and healing – these are among the common phrases used. The different rationales of different systems have different goals, but all of them use language which is difficult to follow, they say, until the path has actually been followed in practice.

Who has tried it? How can I trust it?
Millions upon millions of people who have not been content only to skim over their lives.

☐ After the PERSIANS came the HINDUS; they developed the elaborate practices of Yoga which still survive. Different yogic routines claim different emphases, but essentially they all aim to overcome suffering and pain and to bring control over the cravings of the senses.

☐ The JEWISH author of the book of Job, well before the birth of Christ, exclaims, 'O if only you would be silent, you would learn wisdom.'

☐ The STOICS in Greece wanted to surmount material

preoccupations and deny the body by raising their mental powers in a search for purity. They strongly influenced the HERMITS who went into the desert to meditate.

☐ By the sixth century AD the growing CHRISTIAN movement had produced mystics, particularly in Greece and Egypt, who are still honoured today.

☐ Also around this time the teachings of BUDDHA were spreading. His teachings about the 8-fold path to Perpetual Bliss spread quickly throughout China, Tibet and Thailand, encouraging men to believe they were all equally able to achieve detachment from the pains of this world and an extinguishing of all their desires.

☐ Meanwhile CHRISTIANITY was developing its own schools of meditation and contemplation: pain and suffering were not to be denied or avoided but to be offered as paths to growth – crucifixion followed by resurrection. Christ has been there before and provides the strength and power needed to cope with suffering if he is allowed entry.

☐ In the twentieth century there has been an enormous spread of interest in the *techniques* of meditation, sometimes divorced from any religious content. In particular Transcendental Meditation has spread to every country in the world – except perhaps Russia. TM seeks to empty the passions.

☐ A blend of East/West technique is now used by many modern therapists, especially in forms of visualization and auto-genics.

So the path to inner stillness is both well-tried and well-trod. The difference today is the way in which technique and content or goal have become separated. The exploration and discovery of what goes on inside oneself is a fascinating one; how much it remains a journey of self-knowledge and how much it becomes an opening up to power that is external to oneself, and whether that power is named as 'Christian' or not, is very much the choice of the individual.

★　★　★　★　★

A common finding today, that often remains unexpressed until the possibilities are framed by someone else, is a hunger for silence. Perhaps it is a reaction to the noise and movement and challenge of our daily living, but the eagerness with which ordinary people take to silence when given a chance is very striking. Many searching people find that sharing silence in a group has special advantages: each person can use it in their own way, following where their spirit leads them, but gaining strength and support and 'normality' from their common stillness.

How is it done?
By using quiet, and imagination, and mental focusing.

What happens in the quiet depends largely on the goal.

It is very helpful to spend a few minutes *'centering down'* while immediate and pressing concerns are gently put on one side. Some people find it useful to concentrate on their breathing; every 'out' breath gets rid of used-up air, exhausted thoughts, negative feelings. Every 'in' breath takes in new enabling air, fresh 'inspiration'. Gradually the breathing quietens, and becomes deeper and slower and from the diaphragm, until it is so low one ceases to be conscious of it.

There are five steps to stillness:

1. Stillness of my muscles and body. Relaxation techniques can help.
2. Stillness of my chatter, both of my tongue and in my mind.
3. Stillness of my thoughts, a focusing down on to one picture,
   or one theme,
   or one object,
   or one word.

4. Stillness in the here and now, neither in the past nor the future,
5. Stillness with God.

★　★　★　★　★

Distractions don't matter as much as those who worry over them think they do. It's the singleness of mind, the focused intent, that is important.

> Come gently to the one thought; if red herrings come into the picture don't chase them, or get irritated by them, or even react to them at all. Let them swim out again just as easily as they came in – rather like when you are watching the bubbles rise in an aquarium, the fish are quite happy darting in and out of your view, they will still be there to attend to when you have completed the job of counting the bubbles, but for the moment they are not your concern. The bubbles are.

Some types of meditation depend upon *watching:*

☐ Watching what happens to my own senses when I am still, heightening my own awareness of what is happening around me: the sounds, smells, tastes, pressures, feel, of all those things with which I am in contact but whose messeages are usually overlaid. The Buddhists say that with practice I will hear a fly move behind me.

☐ Watching with the imagination what happens in a particular historical scene, perhaps an incident from the gospels. What is the lesson it holds for me and my way of life?

☐ Watching what my imagination does with a particular story – a theme or a fantasy – from which I can learn about the images that the deepest part of my personality wants to send me. These are always significant; what is it I need to understand *now?*

☐ Watching the logical steps – or the intuitive steps – that come to me when I look at a particular situation in my present life. If I approach it stripped, like an onion, of all the preconceptions, prejudices,

presumptions I usually carry around, I will probably
be surprised at the steps I am led into.

Into this watching type of meditation also comes *Visualization* – a way of focusing mental and imaginative powers either on to a familiar scene which restores peace and serenity and joy to my life when it has become dry and drained and despairing, or on to an object in a way that is increasingly being used as a therapy by healers.

Some methods of meditation depend upon *listening:*

☐ Here the main idea is a bit different. I want to empty my mind and senses as completely as possible because these things can get in the way of listening. So I want to reduce the clutter around me and leave all my baggage outside.

☐ It involves stripping off all the layers we protect ourselves with during ordinary personal contacts. Rather like preparing to sunbathe, each item of clothing – or image-making or disguise – has to drop away until the unprotected and exposed self can really bask. And listen.

☐ Some people cultivate this technique by disciplining everything to the contemplation of one image – it may be a dot on the wall or one sound, it may be one syllable.

☐ Others take one phrase – it may be 'God is love' or 'My peace I give you' or any short mantra from the Scriptures or similar work concerning things of the spirit – and hold it quietly, repeating it and nothing else, until it gives up depths of meaning unguessed at before. This deep listening can reveal insights that carry through ordinary living for years.

☐ Some empty themselves in order to stay empty, and 'clean and swept'; others, including Christians, empty themselves in order to be filled. What Christians find they are filled with is from a source beyond their reckoning, from a warmth and strength and love that is inexhaustible; from a creative power that always surprises. The gift and the energy and the goodwill is never-ending; it is only my capacity and willingness to receive it that is limited.

Most forms of meditation and contemplation have as their goal an increased understanding of things of the spirit. Where practitioners differ is whether they are seeking the spirit of their own personhood, an un-named 'other' spirit, or the Holy Spirit. The techniques involved in any of these searches may be very similar, but the content and the direction will be very different. In all cases, however, these techniques will need a teacher or companion before too long, a pilot who can help to avoid the voids.

> If I dive too deep by myself I will stir up the mud at the
> bottom of the pool, or touch the voids that can be
> violent, or just find an emptiness that enervates me. Or
> I may mix up the value of recognizing my true feelings
> with false emotionalism. But in company with a guide –
> or better still with Christ as guide – these hazards
> themselves increase my felt knowledge, and I will be
> affirmed as I am steered through them.

There is a level beyond which logic and reason are inadequate. Some things are so un-knowable and so un-speakable that the very attempt to squeeze them into a framework of knowledge and words lessens them. The only way of comprehending them is to experience them for oneself. The unfailing test to apply to any of these experiences is to ask afterwards:
'Was that experience growth-full?
in-spiriting?
have I got somewhere?' or
'Was that experience undermining?
dis-spiriting?
am I more lost?'

By using the techniques of meditation and contemplation I can get in touch with depths which are unfathomable within myself, or heights that are limitless of the Other, the Creator. The constriction between these two immensities is where I am *now*. Inevitably, these two are in touch with one another, so whichever way I reach, my own spirit will expand. I only inhibit the availability of the immensities by inhibiting my own approach to them. This can be expressed figuratively like this:

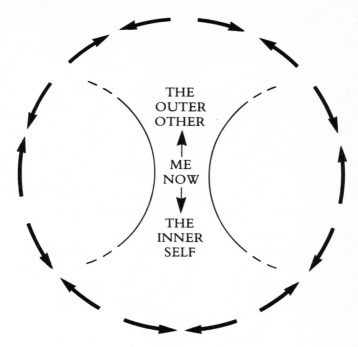

THE
OUTER
OTHER

↑
ME
NOW
↓

THE
INNER
SELF

A salt doll journeyed for thousands of miles over land, until it finally came to the sea. It was fascinated by this strange moving mass, quite unlike anything it had ever seen before.

'Who are you?' said the salt doll to the sea.

The sea smilingly replied, 'Come in and see.'

So the doll waded in. The further it walked into the sea the more it dissolved, until there was only very little of it left. Before that last bit dissolved, the doll exclaimed in wonder, 'Now I know what I am!'*

★ ★ ★ ★ ★

* Anthony de Mello, *The Song of the Bird*, G. S. P. Anand, Gujarat, 1984, p. 98.

It has been said that the rewards of meditation and contemplation are so great that they can become self-indulgent unless they end with some form of resolution. How it affects my behaviour depends upon the ethical foundation to my life.

———CHRISTIAN OUTLOOK———

This chapter has been all about ways of strengthening wholeness – all of wholeness, so a balance is kept – keeping our bodies strong, our minds stimulated, our feelings aware, and our spirits nurtured. Perhaps the fact that Jesus Christ found time to feed his spirit isn't so surprising. After all, you may say, he was primarily a spiritual leader, one would expect him to nurture the spirit. But the really surprising thing about Jesus Christ was the balance he kept in his ordinary life.

☐ He didn't give up social drinking and eating like his cousin John the Baptist did.
☐ He didn't escape indefinitely into the desert to study and pray like the Essenes in the Qumran hermit community did.
☐ He didn't let his ideals run away into political catastrophies like the zealots did.

Instead he joined in the feasting and celebrations of his neighbours – for which he was criticized by the Pharisees at the time.

He gleaned his teaching from his observation of the life around him, as he lived it with his fellow men.

Christ slept, ate, drank, socialized like the rest of us.
IN WHAT WAS HE DIFFERENT? . . .

Part Three

COMMON SITUATIONS OF STRESS

This section is quite different.

It is designed as a collection of 'tips'; suggestions and hints about how the previous discussion can be applied to particular positions of stress. They are only pointers in certain directions, you will have to work out the details and find the path that suits you best yourself.

Some of the 'tips' could equally well fit in other situations – see how *you* would redistribute them. This particularly applies to the 'coping phrases' which are peppered throughout the chapters. We all have our own short-cuts in language, quick formulas that get us through trying moments. The ones provided here have been collected over a considerable time, and they are offered as a means of sparking off your own consciousness of your own coping phrases. If you have prepared such formulas of your own before a testing crisis, you will find they are ready at hand for you to use to convince yourself without too much extra thought. For centuries people have found the well-tried legends such as 'Every cloud has a silver lining' and 'A trouble shared is a trouble halved' and 'A bird in the hand is worth two in the bush' reassuring in practice; some of them are good at turning negatives into positives. Now find some of your own.

11
Waiting

Why put waiting *first?*

Most people, most days, have to cope with periods of waiting:

waiting in queues,
waiting for the train,
waiting for an appointment,
waiting for an answer,
waiting for a meal,
waiting at the traffic lights,
waiting for a delivery, for confirmation,
for news, for . . .

For many people waiting can be almost torture; for most of us it means at least frustration; for some of us it only means boredom. For all of us it means we aren't getting what we want, so we are feeling thwarted. We want to go, to get it, to have it, to get on with it. Energy gets pent up, tension rises, tempers get frayed, and 'others' get the blame. Events are outside our control, and yet it is we ourselves who will have to bear the consequences . . . It's all so unfair.

When the waiting ends, if we're lucky, we'll experience a flood of relief. Too often these days, when we are constantly being reminded of our *rights*, it is more likely that aggression levels will have risen too far. Then my elbow will push others just too rudely, my resentment will flare out just too quickly, my foot will press down on the accelerator just too forcibly, and a chain of irritation starts which may lead to rows and accidents.

SO WHAT TO DO?

This patch of waiting, however unwanted, is an extra bonus of time. Perhaps it is unexpected, not bargained for, but nonetheless it is there. The question is, how to make the best use of it, rather than the worst use of it.

Use this chance, don't waste it.

STRESS-SKILLS FOR THOSE WHO WAIT

☐ *Planning*. Use the time to make lists, to order the jobs for the day with readjusted timing, to mentally work through a problem.

What is the biggest hurdle ahead in your life? Take this chance to visualize the hiccups; run through how it would go at it's *best*. Take time to have a proper look at something that has been neglected and needs thinking about.

☐ *Awareness*. If your life is already in order, use the time for an awareness exercise.

What am I feeling right now? Is all my fret really justified? Is there another way round it? What am I seeing, hearing, touching, smelling, what can I learn from what my body is telling me? How are other people near me feeling?

Put your energy into looking at something you wouldn't ordinarily have time to get into: follow the grain of wood near you, watch a spider, imagine the dancing specks in the air – you will find another world going on around you that is quite unperturbed and unrattled by the fact that you are waiting.

Practise a relaxation body-scan.

☐ *Positive thinking*. What is there in this situation that is enjoyable?

Not having to rush at the moment? The colours around me? The smiles I get by chatting to those next to me? The kick I get from realizing I needn't let the frustration get to me?

De-light is a good word – it not only implies pleasure, but also the lightening of a heavy situation, and the lighting-up of a dark situation.

☐ *Understanding*. Play the part of the devil's advocate and put yourself into the shoes of whoever you think is causing the wait.

> It not only stretches the imagination – sometimes! – it also makes the time pass easily and the stress much easier for me to bear; so it is being easy on myself as well as perhaps being easy on the source of the waiting.

☐ *Humour*. Talk to the person who is in the queue behind you – they must have even longer to wait!

CHRISTIAN OUTLOOK

Wherever there is a scrap of undistracted time, there is the opportunity to reinforce our sense of the presence of Christ, really to be aware of it as a present reality. Then in this presence, to offer to him the upturned timetable, the frustration, the other people involved, the various outcomes of the delay. He will know best what to do with them.

12
Worry and anxiety

It is a significant fact that the more affluent and secure a society becomes, the more its members are likely to be burdened by worry and anxiety. In societies where catastrophe is a common experience, daily worry and anxiety are less of a preoccupation.

Today we are bugged by the fact that we are so security conscious. We have security locks and security caps; security systems and security dogs; security projects in schools and security guards in our homes. We are secured by national insurance and private insurance, life insurance and health insurance; we are offered insurance against mishap for our houses, our goods, cars, education, travel, pets and particular parts of our bodies. With so much effort and money being poured into ensuring that we are 'safe', safety has become a national obsession, and it is hardly surprising that an opposite effect has surfaced, that of anxiety. A large section of our population feel eaten up with worry. It's as though vast numbers of people have been encouraged to expect a malign outcome that will pounce at the least hint of an unprotected chink in their lives.

Some people can take it all in their stride and wonder what all the fuss is about. They remain unmoved by the malevolent watchers in the wings and they can become impatient with those who remain more sensitive to terrible possibilities. The Trusters may try to rationalize the situation with the Mistrusters, quoting statistics of improbability and scoffing at imagined disasters. But worriers worry, and it is seldom much use telling them not to. People who worry would do anything to drop their burden of anxiety, and hearing others insist that 'there is nothing to worry about' just makes them feel even more depleted.

> Maybe it is that the worrier has a need to worry as part of his make-up; if this immediate cause for worry were to be taken away another would take its place. Maybe the realization of this would itself be of more help to a worrier than all the reassurances of 'there's no point in worrying' that they are so frequently offered.

One thing is for sure: no one wants to drop the weight of worry from the worrier's shoulders more than the worrier himself. Worry is a highly distressing business, and it is a fallacy to imagine that anyone worries in order to get attention. The state of disturbance and turbulence endured by anxious people is both exhausting and debilitating; any hint of recrimination about their being anxious merely adds insult to their already raw injury.

It's only too easy for those who do not carry this burden to switch off; very likely there is no need for such a degree of anxiety; very likely it is the state of the worrier rather than the circumstances themselves that are a cause for concern; very likely it does feel like a no-win situation, but these are no reasons to withdraw sympathy from the worrier. He/she will need all the support they can get.

SO, WHAT TO DO?

STRESS-SKILLS FOR THOSE WHO WORRY

☐ Allow the worry, don't fight it or try to deny it.

> Try to recognize whether it is just the circumstances themselves or my own vulnerability which makes me so disturbed. How have I reacted before? If this is a fairly familiar state to be in, and things worked out before quite well after all, maybe it is not the situation itself that is so awful but just my perception of it. Perhaps it is easier for me to cope with me and how I feel, than with outside circumstances over which I have less control.

☐ If there are things to be done which will improve the

situation (ringing a friend, leaving the light on, arranging an appointment with a professional helper) these should be done; having done them I must try to deal with my own emotions.

Having allowed, admitted the worry and done all that is objectively advisable to deal with it, I will try to wrap it up in a parcel and leave it outside my door just for the moment so I can relax. I know it won't go away and it will still be there when I have to go back to it, but just for a little while I put it on one side.

☐ When there is little more to be done, I will make a space to relax. Distraction – such as going shopping or to the theatre – may help, but deep relaxation will effect more.

Practising deep muscular relaxation together with the technique of *visualization* can work wonders. While my body is still and quiet and warm, I think of a special place of peace and content that I have experienced before. It may be only for five minutes at a time at first, but gradually I will be able to reach this place more frequently and for longer periods. Perhaps 'he's got the whole world in his hands', might help.

☐ I survived before, so I will survive again.

The periods of trust will lengthen, they will get stronger. I will cope better with attacks of worry, it will lose its hold on me if I am patient. Then I will have reached a greater wholeness than if I had never been troubled.

─────CHRISTIAN OUTLOOK─────

Many worriers find that the phrase, 'Lord have mercy on me,' carries particular strength. In effect it is saying:

I know I am in need,
I know I need consoling,
I am aware that I find it difficult to trust:

Where a need is acknowledged – Christ will fill it!

In the beatitudes he was saying, 'Blessed are those who are aware of their need . . .'

The word 'mercy' derives from the Greek word for oil: in symbolic terms

oil brings *healing* – it is used to pour into wounds to soften the pain and heal the raw edges;

oil brings *anointing* – it is used to proclaim a person's uniqueness;

oil brings *commissioning for a new start* – it is used in initiation ceremonies, sending the initiated one out with blessing and power.

Kyrie Eleison – 'Christ, I am in need of the blessing of your oil; I acknowledge that I want your healing, anointing and commissioning. Christe Eleison.'

13
Panic

It is characteristic that those who are attacked by panic think they are on their own. It seems that everyone else is composed, controlled, and has obviously got everything well in hand; I am the only one who dreads boarding the plane, entering the crowded room, who loses the essential files, forgets the essential dates. *Am I really?*

We are *all* adept at composing masks, and from the first time a parent did not respond to our rawly exposed emotion in the way we had expected, we started hiding behind our faces. Although society allows us to cover our heads and bodies if we want to, our faces are always left exposed. By the time we become adults we have become adept, through painful experience, at adjusting our faces to display only what we think other people want to see.

So it is a fallacy that I am the only one feeling this panic, just because others aren't showing theirs. However, it is true that I am left to cope with it privately, on my own. Others too are left to cope with theirs, because panic is extraordinarily catching, and for the sake of the majority the ordinary rule is to leave an individual in a panic severely alone. The pressure is therefore on me not to show what I am feeling and even, if possible, to deny it altogether.

That's where the trouble begins, clamping down on my feelings even when they are screaming to get out. As I clamp down on my negative behaviour, I also clamp down on my positive coping behaviour. This means that I am likely either to freeze, or to rush around madly trying to distract the panic from overwhelming me. Neither of these patterns are particularly productive; but when an abyss is about to gape open in front of me I cannot think straight. So it is helpful to have at hand a specific tactic I can rely on when a panic is drawing close. This tactic has to be thoroughly convincing and therefore has to be practised beforehand so that it can come to mind as soon as it is needed.

Each individual has to try out and establish their own; the following ideas have proved to be of use to many, but *they won't all apply to every one.*

STRESS-SKILLS for PANIC

Breathing out
SIGH *OUT* all unwanted,
   used up,
      exhausted air;
         . . .let it go, get rid of it,
           EXPEL IT!

You may find yourself trying hard to take IN more breath than you can hold. Concentrate instead on letting it OUT. Air will come in automatically; it doesn't have to be controlled consciously. Your lungs will fill with good, enabling, fresh air, using the reflexes governed by the respiratory centre in the brain; so you can concentrate on letting your chest wall relax, letting its weight fall with the gravity that pulls it, and allowing all the expired air to take with it all the unwanted negativity. Feel the relief of getting rid of that lot!

Objective reasoning
Some times, some people, and not all people at all times, find it helpful to look the situation in the face and work out what could be the worst thing that could happen. How would the worst situation be taken care of? Who could be called on for help? How would it resolve? If you can see yourself managing in those circumstances, then the present one may not seem so bad. If this is a type of rationalization that works for you, well and good: but if it gives occasion

for your imagination to run riot, then leave it well alone. (Confrontation therapy should be left to professional therapists who can handle it successfully, unless it comes 'naturally' to you.)

Panic Tactic
PAUSE   just hold it for a split second . . .

Absorb your feelings, allow them, don't get rigid denying them;

Unblock; this is the point of a U-turn. As you allow and admit a bit of your bad feelings, you can also allow and admit a bit of your ordinary coping powers; as you unblock them, you will find you can –

Start steadily somewhere; anywhere, something small, one small step you can succeed with; then

Expand; go with it, gradually, gently, let it flow.
    Flowing not Fraughting

Coping phrases
Have at hand a phrase, like a jingle, you can hang on to and put your trust in. You may already have found something useful in this way, or you may come across one of your own in the future. Meanwhile, these are suggestions that have been good for others:

'I survived before, I'll survive again.'
'By tomorrow we'll all be laughing.'
'The stars will stay in their courses whatever happens.'
'What goes up, must come down.'

————CHRISTIAN OUTLOOK————

Thinking of 'coping phrases', there are multitudes of them in the psalms that have helped people through bad times down the centuries. A particularly powerful one comes from the writings of Dame Julian, the fourteenth-century anchorite who lived in astonishingly restrictive circumstances:

> *'All shall be well,*
> *And all shall be well,*
> *And all manner of thing shall be well.*
> *The blessed Trinity shall make all well that is not well'.*

Or, more simply:

> *'Underneath are the everlasting arms'.*

14

Sleeplessness

There has been an enormous amount of research into our sleeping habits and needs over the last decade, and there have been some surprising results. A common finding has been that lack of sleep itself causes no problems to the body, but it is *our worry over lack of sleep* that causes the problems.

The current record for controlled sleeplessness in laboratory conditions is 205 hours! That is, the human volunteers who were well fed, well warmed, and well occupied, kept awake for more than eight full 24-hour periods! This makes our two or three hour wakefulness look rather insignificant.

Nevertheless, most of us are not in controlled laboratory conditions, nor are we young volunteers in the prime of life. Our wakefulness leaves us feeling thoroughly pulled down. How do we cope with this? A good beginning is to rationalize the difficulty:

The experts claim that:

- [ ] the *BODY* needs *REST*, stillness, cessation from movement, more than extended sleep; and that
- [ ] the *MIND* needs *REM* – that is, rapid eye-movement, very deep sleep, which lasts only about two hours in any one night. This is the time during which our dreams take place and deep levels of unconsciousness take over from our daily consciousness. Without this particular type of sleep we quickly become irritable and mentally disorganized, but on the other hand it is this type of sleep that will 'get in first' if we have a short night.

It would seem that as long as we allow our bodies to lie still and relaxed, it is healthier to ENJOY the peace and quiet of lying awake than to exhaust ourselves emotionally by fretting about it. In fact, sleeplessness appears to have no effect whatever on any of our normal body functions. The volunteers in the experiments referred to above were fully restored after only one night's proper sleep. (It's different if people are simultaneously deprived of food and warmth and drink and peace of mind. There must be no confusion here with those who suffer at the hands of hostile interrogators, for instance.)

> The lesson is that no one becomes ill simply through
> lack of sleep, although the *worry* of being unable to
> sleep causes many people considerable stress and anxiety.
> With this reassuring fact behind us, how should we
> manage those seemingly endless periods of sleeplessness
> that we dread?

The actual *routine* we establish for going to bed is very important; there are some simple recommendations to help:

- ☐ It should start at least 1½ hours before we hope to go to sleep.
- ☐ Gradually slow down, reducing energy output; so strong physical exercise or mental stimulation should be avoided.
- ☐ For some people late night television should be reduced.
- ☐ Eat some starchy food, such as biscuits or sandwiches, so the stomach isn't empty – fourteen hours is a long fast for a 'worried' digestion.
- ☐ Background music, calm rather than stimulating, is a help.
- ☐ A hot drink (but not tea, coffee, or cocoa, which all contain the stimulant caffeine) is good. Herbal teas, fruit juices, soup or yeast extract, and milky drinks are all preferable to alcohol immediately before sleep. Alcohol may appear at first to make one sleepy, but this effect wears off after about four hours and then it has dehydrating and diuretic properties which come into play and disturb sleep.

- ☐ A hot leisurely bath is helpful.
- ☐ A definite routine over the chores of clearing and locking up: turning out – lights and fires and cookers and cats! – in a regular order at a regular time avoids any unnecessary anxiety that these essentials have not been done.
- ☐ Have a pad and pencil by the bedside to jot down those ideas which may keep you awake if they get forgotten.
- ☐ Some people like to practise easing relaxation exercises before getting into bed.
- ☐ A good book, one without too much stimulation, or more especially reading poetry, is a great help.
- ☐ Now, wrap up your worries and concerns, and objectify them – there is nothing more you can do about them until the morning. So put them firmly into a paper bag and leave them under your pillow. They will be quite safe there until you retrieve them in the morning.

Some people who find difficulty in getting to sleep may do better going to bed later, when they are more tired. Some who find difficulty returning to sleep having woken up, may find it better to go to bed *earlier* in order to get more sleep in before they wake up. Either way, make a regular habit and stick to it.

If, having made all these preparations, there are still wakeful periods in the night, what to do then?

STRESS-SKILLS FOR WAKEFULNESS

- ☐ Enjoy it! Savour the peace, the quiet, the restfulness, the freedom from demands, the soft velvet darkness.

- ☐ Get up *before* you get worried about being unable to get back to sleep again. Make a drink and plan a task to be done that is easy and satisfying – writing a letter, singing a narrative song to yourself, stroking the cat, putting a troubling (or exciting) thought down on paper, reaching a decision. When the task is completed, slip back into bed without fuss but aware of your satisfaction at having *done* something.

☐ Visualize a pleasant, familiar, contented scene from your past life that was safe and happy but not wildly exciting. Hold it, climb into it, go carefully over every detail in the picture, stay with its contentment. If other present anxieties disturb you, just tell them quietly they will get their proper attention in the morning but that they are out of place right now, and creep back into your picture.

☐ Sometimes the contentment just won't stay, and you need something to hold your wandering thoughts in the present. Practise breathing with your stomach, pushing it gently up and down using your diaphragm to breathe with rather than your chest walls. This will give your other respiratory muscles a well-earned rest, and give your mind something that has no great importance on which to concentrate.

☐ A simple relaxation routine can be very helpful:

Think of a rolling, massaging warmth spreading over your body melting all its knots of tension as it goes. Starting with your forehead, it relaxes your cheeks, jaw, neck, and then goes rolling down over your shoulders, chest and abdomen. It brings softness and heaviness as it goes. This massaging wave of relaxation rolls down your arms, hands and fingers so they become warm and heavy and limp. It passes on over your pelvic floor and all its organs relax, and then down your thighs, knees, calves which get soft and spreading and heavy. Finally your hard working feet and toes melt in softness and warmth, and you are totally relaxed all over. Enjoy the easiness and looseness and space in your resting body.

Remind yourself that a period of deep relaxation brings three or four times more release to toned muscles than ordinary sleep.

☐ A student found that the surest way of sending himself to sleep was to insist to himself that the last thing he really wanted to do was to go to sleep! He certainly didn't waste energy worrying about being awake.

It's doubtful if you and your body can resist all these persuasions . . .

————CHRISTIAN OUTLOOK————

The old-fashioned habit of praying by the bedside last thing at night is probably a stronger reassurance than all the other recommendations put together. Placing my self and my body and all my concerns into the hands and care of the Creator, knowing full well that he will have oversight of them all night, and will return them regenerated in the morning, is an act of trust that cannot be over-stated.

The French theologian/poet Peguy, wrote of the abandonment we all undergo when giving ourselves up to the total un-control of sleep. *'What more can I want than that the absolute power that organizes and holds and nurtures the entire universe is prepared to accept my abandonment into his own hands?'*

15
Nervous habits

The sort of habits that lie in the context of a book about stress such as this are those little bits of constantly repeated behaviour that seem to be able to prop us up when we are feeling anxious. We are conscious of them but nonetheless we find them peculiarly difficult to control. Silly things like foot-swinging, giggling, nail-biting, continually rechecking, as well as some of the more health-damaging habits such as smoking and over-eating. There are also the reflexes that we are aware of but which are not yet part of our conscious behaviour, such as facial twitches and irritating gestures; also to be included here is the hidden subject of stress-incontinence. Actual stress phobias are not in this list, for they need more professional help than the do-it-yourself techniques which follow.

At first sight it is surprising that such a varied list of habits could have anything in common, but there are basic principles which fit any attempt to look at and change our own behaviour. It is worth taking them seriously and then experimenting with them to see how far they can apply to each habit, and to my own in particular.

STRESS-SKILLS for ALTERING HABITS

☐ *Taking a good look straight at it!*
Don't whitewash over it; when do I do it? Do I know why? What *bad* effect does it have? On whom? Does it make me look worse and feel better? Would I rather look as better as I feel? How badly do I *want* to change? (If the

answer to that is 'not much' then there's no point in reading further.)

☐ *Make a firm decision about wanting to change something*
Tell someone about wanting to change. Tell them how you propose to go about it. If they are not sure that you can, determine to show them!

☐ *Set up small goals*
– ones you know you can reach, such as: growing one fingernail for a week; putting a stool near your foot in the evening so you will be made aware when you kick it; keeping your cigarette packet in a drawer upstairs so you will have to fetch it. You yourself can work out the ploys that will help you to become just that bit more aware of your habit, and the habit just that little bit more difficult to practise.

☐ *Arrange small rewards for yourself.*
What gives you really strong motivation? Showing off to someone else how well you have done? Putting a small sum into a box to build up to a larger sum for a specific goal – buying something you really want, giving to your favourite charity, planning a celebration. Or even the simple, powerful act of patting yourself on the back and raising your own worth in your own eyes.

☐ *Surprise yourself!*
Perhaps this is the best part of all, realizing that you *can* do it, after you had only *hoped* you could do it.

When you catch yourself saying to yourself, 'You're really no good, you know you really can't do it. It has never worked for you before. You're so weak it's not even really worth trying' – just think, would you speak to your own child like that? . . . Then reword those phrases as if you were speaking to a child, the child inside you that is still there but too often gets squashed out. Cosset yourself a little, make your expectations of yourself more realistic, be gentle and patient with yourself for a while. You will get better results from yourself in the end.

And then tackle the next goal. Another step, one rung further on.

Another example of how we can heal ourselves is epitomized in the following approach to a very upsetting, private, undiscussed complaint. This is a nervous response that has been described as one of the last hidden subjects of our society. It is extremely common – it might even affect every woman at some stage of her life – and is very distressing.

Stress Incontinence
It is because stress incontinence is so little discussed generally that many woman feel there is nothing to be done about it. There is plenty to be done about it, and most of it is very practical. There are, of course, a minority of cases where medical treatment is essential, and in most cases a doctor's check-up is advisable; but for the vast majority of women who put up with acute feelings of bladder incompetence there are ways in which they can help themselves using only common sense reponses.

1. *Using logic:*
Arrange the day in such a way that a toilet will be accessible at regular intervals – say every two or three hours (more frequently if need be at first).

Remember that a large amount of fluid taken at one time will need to be got rid of within about 1½ hours, so if you leave the house at 9 a.m., have breakfast around 7.30 a.m. Smaller amounts of liquid can be held for longer.

The bladder is made up of muscle that is enormously elastic. It *can* cope with a lot of fluid. It is *our worry* that it can't cope which makes it tighten and constrict so we feel it cannot expand. (What an astonishing metaphor of how we treat ourselves!)

2. *Using practical know-how*, when the need to empty seems very urgent:

The bladder is a small balloon inside the larger, tougher, bag called the abdominal cavity. Think of a shopping bag with several things inside it, and at the bottom there is the partly inflated balloon. If the outside walls of the shopping bag are soft and allowed to stretch, there will be more room for the balloon inside to get bigger. If the opening at the top of the bag is left open a bit, again there will be less pressure on the balloon at the bottom.

To put this imagined picture into practice, means several adaptations:

(a) Breathe *out*, so the diaphragm which is the ceiling of the abdominal cavity lifts and relieves the pressure inside it.

(b) Push the front walls of the abdomen *out* (at this moment looking slim is of minor importance) so that there is a greater space inside.

(c) Try to imagine the two circular muscles at the outlet of the bladder which each draw tight to prevent an inadvertent loss of fluid; if you can relax the *internal* muscle, this too will relieve the pressure. The external muscle will hold on its own, for a short while.

(d) Avoid carrying heavy weights, since this too presses down on the top of the bladder, squeezing it and making it feel it needs to burst.

3. *Specific exercises*

All the organs within the abdominal cavity are supported by a sling of muscles. This sling is attached to bone low down at the front of the body and passes between the thighs and up to the base of the spine. This is known as the pelvic floor, and the openings from the bladder, vagina and rectum are all contained within it. Once the feel of this group of muscles is recognized, it is quite easy to exercise by tensing and relaxing it. A good way of doing this is to squeeze the muscles as if to stop the bladder or rectum emptying, but even better is learning to pull them upwards and inwards as if drawn towards the navel. Sometimes it helps to imagine a £5 note being held in the cleft and not allowing it to be taken away!

These are isometric exercises that can be done at any time, standing or sitting or lying down, without any movement being observable. It is only a matter of remembering to do them.

4. *Convince yourself,*
 My body can cope if I let it.
 My body has an automatic control of its own; I can only make things worse by trying to over-ride its efficiency. It needs my trust and not my doubt. Just take the strain off it, *and it will cope.*

These suggestions take only a little space on the page, but they need a considerable amount of time and patience to put into effect. Don't give up too easily, they are probably going against all your usual habits of keeping your tummy in and breathing with your chest. You will still be doing those things most of the time, just adapt your practice when the need to empty your bladder is urgent. Rehearse the ideas at home, so you will feel more confident when you go out.

 . . . *It can be done* . . .

All 'nervous habits' need time and patience and the conviction that changing them is worthwhile. And you need to keep hope alive.

──────CHRISTIAN OUTLOOK──────

Hope is one of the three major Christian virtues; not justice or equality or my rights or many of the high-profile aims which are so righteously vaunted in our present-day publicity, but *hope*. It often gets exercised in small, unseen, unsung ways in the privacy of people's hearts and homes. It can grow in matters that are small and nationally trivial, and the more it is exercised the greater it will grow. This germinal hope is the greatest *hope* for our world.

 Small goals achieved can soon grow into larger ones, and then greater, and continue without diminishing.

'We have a strong encouragement to take a firm grip on the hope that is held out to us' (Heb. 6:18).

'Our Lord Jesus Christ . . . has given his love and . . . inexhaustible comfort and sure hope to strengthen you in everything good that you do or say' (2 Thess. 2:16–17).

What am I hoping for? . . . *where is Christ leading me?*

16

Loneliness

Loneliness is far more common and far more poignant than many of us like to think. When we do consider it, we tend to think of loneliness as something to be afraid of, to avoid, something which causes intractable problems and which we don't like to admit in ourselves. But loneliness doesn't only happen to other people, and loneliness is not only attached to people who are solitary. No one is secure from loneliness; it affects single people, married people, children and especially elderly people. There are differences in the amount of time people spend in being solitary, and the degree to which they actually enjoy being solitary, but loneliness itself is with all of us. The stress that it brings differs enormously; it can vary from being just uncomfortable sometimes, to being something that is nearer anguish most of the time. At all times, those who are lonely need consideration, but the sort of consideration that actually does something, and isn't only a mawkish sympathy.

One can be as lonely in a crowd as on a wastelend. Or as contented on one's own as at a party. The difference lies between loneliness and *aloneness*. Aloneness is something to be highly prized, even coveted, and it is certainly worth protecting, but the stress of loneliness can become so engrossing that it overlooks the positives of aloneness.

Loneliness takes many forms, and it can be found in every place and every occupation. People are naturally gregarious and on the whole we live and work in groups; when such arrangements don't work out we react with hurt, bewilderment and anger. With various other emotions this all adds up to the responses of loneliness.

Loneliness has something to do with alienation:

> I feel alien to the crowd I am with . . . the surroundings I am in . . . this sort of talk . . .

> Loneliness also has something to do with not belonging: I yearn for someone to be there . . . someone to like me . . . someone to whom I can . . .

At cut-off points like these the feelings of rejection and separation may be so hurtful and long-standing that they get smothered, and what come across is:

> I don't care . . . I don't want you . . . I'm too good for you anyway . . . I refuse to show myself to you.

* * * * *

When loneliness is totally absorbing it also becomes enervating:

> There's no point in trying . . . It doesn't work.

But there is every point in trying, and then trying some more. Sometimes the dis-comfort and distress of loneliness can act as a spur; this very feeling of being unsettled can spur me on to do something about it. This first group of *stress-skills* comes into this category:

☐ Get out, finding a group to enjoy.
☐ Ask other people in, a neighbour or a colleague from the office.
☐ Do something for someone else. Join a self help group that visits house-bound people whose circumstances are even worse.
☐ Getting a pet can be a great help – there is nothing like coming home to a warm furry welcome.
☐ Having a telephone installed increases a sense of contact with others.

These suggestions may seem obvious, but often they are more easy to suggest than to carry through. Special diffi-culties such as shyness, stammering or having too little confidence in one's physical appearance can turn the simplest social exchange into a momentous hurdle. There are special approaches to help in each of these situations, and a health centre, C.A.B, or library would have local advice to offer. Led small groups can help. Meanwhile the simple procedure of setting a goal, breaking it down into small steps, and planning a means of rewarding yourself can set you well on the way.

★ ★ ★ ★ ★

Whether I am on my own in the physical sense, or on my own in silence, if I stick with it I will discover that to be alone is not necessarily to be lonely. As a child, I looked to my parents and family for a sense of identity, of belonging. As a young adult I probably looked to the acquisition of possessions or qualifications or a job or status for security and indentity. But as I grow older it becomes clearer that my identity and my decisions lie with me, how I behave and respond; clinging on to things or to others to 'say' things for me means I am trying to make them bear a responsibility which finally rests with me alone – with me and my God.

If I can recognize, value, and cherish this uniqueness, this 'own-ness', I will not be lonely because I have something stronger and less clinging to offer others, and they will be attracted to it. Paradoxically, my relationships will be closer because they are freer.

★ ★ ★ ★ ★

All these things are about alleviating the distress of loneliness. But there is another group of stress-skills that are about making the most of the opportunities for aloneness, as least some of the time. These are less widely talked about. They can be carried out together with those in the earlier group, or they may suit those who really dislike socializing, and who really want to make the most of their own company. This second group of skills is quite different. Read it carefully, mull it over, and if it is not for you just pass on. But there may be some to whom these ideas are new, and it may open a new world for them. So draw back the curtains slowly, there is no rush.

> Something happens when you are on your own that can only happen when you are by yourself. It is wordless and cannot be communicated to anyone else – even those you love most dearly. It cannot happen when you are talking with others, because talk uses words. Even music is too exact and too specific.

> Those things that are so close to my inner self I cannot share them with anyone are often unheard, ignored, lost, in the hubbub of family life. The effort to make space for them is too great. But living on my own gives me a chance to listen and mark and inwardly digest those hidden, sparking, movements. One student has called it finding 'the deeper centre of things that are right'. What do you call it?

These inclinations act as undercurrents to our lives whether we discover them or not. Part of the process of reaching such movements is facing the rocks that lie in the way. So we come back yet again to allowing, to admitting, to letting in.

> If I am very taken up with the fact that I am on my own and the fear and hurt that that can bring, I will be unable to see the other possibilities. Once I can look at the situation directly for what it is and resist blaming either myself or others for it, I will be able to accept the position I find myself in with all its advantages as well as its disadvantages. If I can be strong enough to do this, to stay with it, I will learn that I am *not* submerged by what I find, and I have the means to cope with it after all.

> When I have learnt that, I will no longer avoid it, and the emotion itself – as well as the threat of it – will loosen and lose its power.

★　★　★　★　★

Mostly we learn about ourselves by watching the reactions and responses of other people to our behaviour. But we *need aloneness* to learn about that other side of ourselves, our inner workings, what makes us 'tick'. Loneliness is familiar to all of us; no one, even the most gregarious, is a total stranger to it. Those who don't have enough of it have less chance of getting to know that really deep, alone, inner self. People who have little time for attending to that hidden, private, masked, subterranean person will still get by, but will they know what they are missing?

> It isn't until we know ourselves as a SOLE BEING that we can begin to recognize where we are truly comfortable.
> And 'COM-FORT' means with strength, and 'lone' or 'ALONE' come from *ALL ONE*.

————CHRISTIAN OUTLOOK————

Most Christians would feel their sincerest attempts at praying and at knowing themselves (or true self-examination) were on the way to the discovery of their own aloneness. We are all, every one, ultimately alone with God. Our greatest hope is that we shall all, every one, be ultimately at one with God. Many Christians – and increasing numbers of all people – are finding that the way there is made easier by taking some time out to be quiet. Going away from home and friends and family and work and spending time with others, on a few days of stillness, listening. There are over two hundred retreat houses in Great Britain, and even more than that number of open centres, spread throughout the country. These are comfortable houses where both denominational and uncommitted searchers alike spend time getting to know their 'all-one'ness. Have you tried it?

The ancient song puts it:

> *One is one and all alone,*
> *and ever more shall be so.*

17
Relationships*

Relationships . . . Where to start?

Relationships can be the most stressful of all stressors, or be the most rewarding of all our experiences. To make and sustain the best relationships takes our whole: our mind, body, feelings and spirit, but it gives back more, an enriched whole and the gift of the other as well. Unravelling all the ramifications of how this comes about has not yet been done, because we each find our own ways of allowing entry to each other, but the following is offered as a platform for ideas to be teased out and tested, perhaps taken further and followed through with time.

First and foremost,
we are all imperfect.

We *all* need forbearance, I of you and you of me. We are *all* in the same boat needing succour. So why do we act so often as if don't need each other, as if we know all the answers? As if we always know what is best, that we are the only ones who are right, that we are the ones who are in control? Is it to keep ourselves safe? Why is it so important that we should be always safe?

It's such a burden to be right all the time!
The relief of being wrong!
To be relieved of some of that responsibility, it's great! Why do we pretend to hate it so badly?

---

* Caring for children and living with invalids at home will be looked at later. Here the focus is on our relationships with our peers; our colleagues, friends, partners and spouses.

Perhaps if we showed each other a little more often where we felt unsure, insecure, we would find we each *shared* that lack of sureness. And then we could shore up each other's sureness, instead of being so keen to show it up.

★　★　★　★　★

However, there is *always* the other side of the coin.

These days, when there is an emphasis on self-awareness and other-awareness, there is a new risk of becoming so keen on understanding another that this keenness itself becomes intrusive. Some people at some time *want* to share themselves, but it cannot be taken for granted that all people want (or even 'ought') to share themselves at all times. Michael Stancliffe, in his recent book *Symbols and Dances* (SPCK 1987) refers to the fact that 70 per cent of our human communication is non-verbal. He says that total reliance on words 'simply won't do'. He tells of

'persons feeling towards each other,
　gently,
　　caringly,
　　　lovingly, albeit with a certain proper shyness,

as if both persons are sensitive to the fact that when it comes to drawing nearer to another human being one must be marvellously tender, infinitely patient and have endless respect for the other person's integrity.'

If we behave too much like ferrets in our keenness to show understanding and sympathy towards the other – if we try to chase such empathy, dig it out regardless of whether it is welcomed or not – the other person may very well, and not surprisingly, turn into a hedgehog, rolling up into a ball and turning all their prickles outwards.

If I remain quietly cheerful, listening, accepting, and non-argumentative it is more probable that I will grow closer to the ones I wish to get nearer than if I am noisily boisterous, or continuously pessimistic, or attentive mainly to my own activities, and constantly pushing my own viewpoint.

On the whole, it is easier for another person to join

me in an emotion that is expressed in low-key terms, than in one that is over-expressed.

★ ★ ★ ★ ★

Always, all ways, offer respect to the other.
This includes never speaking for the other, or presuming one knows their answer; it is seldom that it can be guessed at realistically.

> It is more fun if I can remain ready to be surprised, than if I act as if I know it all already. And it will be more fun for me too if I can remain ready to encourage the other to be surprising.

It means *enjoying* their point of view, not necessarily feeling threatened or angry because it is different from mine.

> He likes big dogs. I don't, I like small cats. So we have one of each. But he walks the big dog.

It means looking after their sensitivities also, although over-protection itself is a strange thing. Those who do it very often do so out of motives of love and care, but it can turn into a form of disrespect, distrust, of the other's capability for coping, and it may deny them a chance for growth; worse, it may be seen by the one who is being 'protected' as just this.

> I know he can't stand our daughter's new boy-friend. At first I worked quite hard to keep them apart. Then they met by accident at a match; they became very friendly and resented my former 'tact' that had deprived us all.

★ ★ ★ ★ ★

At appropriate times and in appropriate ways I must also respect myself and express my own feelings and needs. There is little point in expecting the other to know or to remember my point of view all the time.

> If I hang back from saying what I feel about things because 'he ought to know . . . he ought to remember . . . I told him before . . .', then I am simply spiting

myself, not him. I won't even get it the way I want, and he will end up feeling injured. No one is perfect; he had other things on his mind when he forgot. A simple reminder will help us both to please the other.

★   ★   ★   ★   ★

Concerning this matter of 'me' and 'you', 'for me' or 'for you', it can touch off so many areas of mistaken pride and remembered put-downs that it's surprising how simple a safety-formula can be. 'We' is more comfortable to bear than 'you' or even 'me'.

Compare:
'It's good to be in contact again: you were very switched off before'; with
'It's good to be in contact again; *we* were very switched-off before'!
or: 'I'll go and lay the table for you'; with
'I'll go and lay the table for *us*'.

Now try applying the change to bigger issues.

★   ★   ★   ★   ★

☐ There is another way of increasing my forbearance of the other while reducing my own angry reaction. It is something that can be of great practical importance to realize, to make real, clearly and quietly. When the other person is a misery, and being a misery to me, it is only a pale reflection of the misery he is going through himself.

☐ When the other one is rude or angry or belligerent or contrary towards me, it is in fact only a portion of the anger and confusion that she is bearing inside towards herself.

☐ *What the other is going through is very much worse than what they are putting me through.*

☐ When I can really get hold of this fact, it becomes much easier and more sensible not to add more misery and anger and conflict to the general turmoil. Perhaps I may even find the means to be comprehending rather than inflammatory in my response, and then the wholeness in both of us can grow.

★　★　★　★　★

Surprisingly, we have been labelled the 'touch-deprived society'. Most cultures allow for physical contact more often and more significantly than the English. If we contact another by touching shoulders, elbows or a hand, or even a bump in the street, it is more likely to set up a train of apologies than one of receptive responses. And yet so much can be said without words, or to reinforce words, if only we would let ourselves. From greeting a stranger into a new organization, or sympathizing with a bereaved person we meet in the street, to offering an unwordy bit of encouragement, there are many small ways in which we could use touch to get our meaning across if only we were a little more free. Words can often be badly chosen and risky, and then a hand contact may be easier; but even when the word is right, physical contact can make it even righter.

In the sexual context, it's good to remember that we have been created with nerve endings in the whole of our skin, and that that skin covers the whole of our bodies. Subtle and sensitive feelings can be communicated between lovers by the use of touch, with or without words, which enrich their relationship with a range of expressing that is endless.

Other ways of using touch are stroking and massaging. These are both techniques recognized to be helpful to people suffering from stress, whether muscular pain or mental strain, and those who want to practise it can either follow their partner's instructions about what eases them best, or follow a community course.

★　★　★　★　★

It is astonishing how slow I can be to learn a simple lesson – whatever way I choose to relate to another, it backfires on me.
For instance:

If I choose to pull him down – I become pulled down myself;
how does that help me?

If I choose to make a judgement about her - I become judged myself:
how does that better me?

If I undermine them – I feel undermined myself:
what good does that do me?

But, if I love, I become loved; if I trust, I become trusted; if I express goodwill, goodwill is returned – you would think my choice would be obvious.

★　★　★　★　★

Many relationships are approached with enormously high expectations, perhaps especially today when each person is left to choose their own friends and partners. We often expect to be totally engrossed in our partner in a way that is largely unrealistic. The ancient Chinese symbol of the yin and yang has been adopted as a proper illustration of how a man and a woman can interlock. This is marvellous for much of the time, but perhaps some adjustment to the figure would allow for more freedom of movement. Over-stretched expectations can cause a lot of harm.

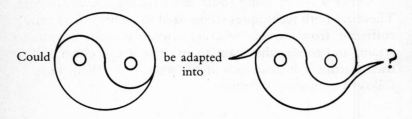

Could [yin-yang symbol] be adapted into [modified yin-yang symbol] ?

Some relationships, including marriage, can work very satisfactorily on the tuning-fork principle. Each partner can follow their own interest or job independently of the other but they really resound when they come together!

170

There are an infinite number of patterns for marriage, probably as many as there are marriages themselves, just as there are an infinite number of sorts of friendships and partnerships. None of them can wisely be compared; each is unique, each is particular. Enjoying and exchanging with each other is different to comparing and competing – we all have a different shape and have to learn different skills to make the best use of them.

There are times when I want, and need, to be dependent upon my friend, my husband, my partner. There are times when I want, and need, to be independent of him. And there are times when he wants, and needs, to be dependent upon or independent of me. A 'good' relationship encompasses all of this, each not weighing too heavily on either. Perhaps it is *interdependence* that is the key.

★　★　★　★　★

All the above are snippets of stress-skills, but it does not add to this section to label them as such. Similarly, they all form part of a Christian outlook on relationships, because relationship is the base and foundation of Christianity's existence. The relationship between the Father, Son, and the Holy Spirit and between the love of that Trinity and me, absorbs the whole of me. It takes up my mind, my body, all my feelings and the whole of my spirit. *And that can be for each of us.*

18
Caring at home for special needs

Those who care for a relative with special needs at home are in a very singular position. On the one hand they are doing one of the most loving and generous jobs it is possible to do, and on the other they can be made to feel demeaned, undervalued and frustrated beyond words. They may find part of their lives is highly rewarding – the one they care for may be sweet-tempered and appreciative and add purpose and companionship where otherwise it was lacking; or, although they don't get any of this, they may find that society as a whole is unwilling to make good their financial sacrifice, or even make up for their emotional drain.

It is not just that the weight of daily caring is heavy – in every sense – or that their own interests and preferences have to come second to those of the cared-for, or even that there is no definite time-limit to the caring; on top of all this there is the personal bewilderment that the best motives and intentions can suddenly turn upside down and become feelings of hostility that are unmentionable, to *anyone*.

There are sources of practical help available in most cases, whether the caring is for a child or spouse or an ageing relative, and whether the disability is physical or mental or both. Local authorities issue lists of addresses and advice about home helps, respite care, benefits, equipment, self-help organizations, and sitters. In whatever ways the stress that is physical is eased, the stress that is emotional seldom gets the attention or release that is needed.

Is any of the following familiar?

'It's not fair! Why should I be the one to put up with all this?'

'I'm so desperately tired, my feelings are emptied, my
mind is dried up from lack of use.'

'They say, "O you can't possibly cope with that", but I
do, and then what happens? I have to cope with some
more, and then they don't even notice!'

'How long is it going to last? If only I could scream at
someone; if I could only *blow* . . .'

'She would have it her way, and now look what's
happened. I knew she couldn't do it all along . . .'

'*If only* it had been different . . .' '*If only* . . .' '*If only* I
hadn't had to give up . . .'

'The perfect child I had planned for . . .' 'The perfect
marriage I had worked for . . .' 'The lovely person
she used to be . . .' 'There is so much to mourn for,
yet there has not been any burial for what isn't any
more . . .'

And the anger and resentment and blame set in, and the
secret need to punish the cared for – which of course must
never be expressed and never happen . . . Then the guilt
which drives me to work harder . . . and get more
exhausted.

How to cope with all this?

STRESS-SKILLS FOR THOSE WHO CARE

If I am a carer, it may be up to me to:

☐ *Protect my own health*. I am the only tool I have to use in
caring, and it is vital I look after my own needs for proper
food, rest, and sleep.

☐ *Find some space for Me*. My own personhood is precious,
as well as that of my relative.

☐ *Find a trusty confidante* to whom I can blow – preferably
another human, but if needs be a cat or a pillow or a
notebook will do until I can reach my friend.

☐ *Develop a sense of objectivity and balance*. I mustn't allow
myself to be set up, to be manipulated into spending

longer or doing more than is necessary, especially when my turn for 'space' comes up. Keeping a sense of proportion about what *really* has to be done for the comfort of my relative is vital in case my own space is eroded.

☐ *Distance myself when viewing the needs of my dependant*, However devoted I am, it is wise to sometimes put on the spectacles of reason, fact and detachment in place of emotional involvement. I may even see where I am not indispensable after all, and my relative may surprise me by coping with certain things for himself.

☐ *Share the responsibility for caring WITH my relative.* It does us both a power of good when the actual 'burden' of care is shared between us. People from outside can be allowed to share in it too, so it becomes a co-operative!

☐ *Encourage a sense of humour*, both in myself and with the one I am caring for. Secret jokes that others aren't part of may help our relationship especially.

☐ *Remember the good times* – perhaps even write them down, not with too much nostalgia, but as fuel to feed me (us) when things are low.

☐ *Plan my rewards.* If the more obvious ones aren't available, perhaps growing things in tubs, making a collection, fantasizing about what I would *really* like, and doing something towards it.

Getting in touch with the appropriate self-help group is perhaps the most constructive thing of all, so that like-minded and like-situated people can share ideas and exchange experiences.

Whenever one is giving a lot *out*, it is essential to have to hand the means of getting refreshed, refurbished. Taking one's own needs seriously is as important as taking the needs of the one who is being cared for seriously. It is hard when you have to do this for yourself, but it is never selfish and *it must be done*.

The rest of us watch your patience and strength in astonishment.

──────CHRISTIAN OUTLOOK──────

Jesus Christ had a knack of seeing the world from the point of view of those who were disadvantaged. He *knew* what it is like to be without. He looked at things from the bottom up.

It can sometimes turn a whole situation turtle if roles are reversed; instead of looking at what I give another person, it is useful to take a look at what that person gives me. It might be a role, an identity, an opportunity to exercise something that otherwise would remain unstretched.

When Christ was thirsty, he asked for water from someone who was herself in need of water; when I am feeling particularly drained, it might be that I can offer the chance of refilling me to the one who has apparently drained me.

It can work, sometimes. *It's called* inter*dependence, and Jesus Christ as a man was particularly practised at it.*

19

Equipping our children

In all ages children have been subject to harmful stresses. Large sections of the child-population have been vulnerable to exploitation, ravaging disease, and early death, Those sources of distress have been replaced by others, and now the stresses are of a different order; children today meet all the confusions of the adult world too early. They are exposed to its pains as well as its pleasures before they have had enough experience of security to buffer them. As a direct result of this turmoil it has become a matter of high priority in the teenage culture to appear cool, desensitized, stress-proofed, and to possess inflated credibility in the street.

To *appear* stress-proofed. But are they?

In reality we have climbing juvenile crime, high addiction rates, increasing alcoholism, a rising rate of suicides, and a vast lack of sense of direction. All these behaviours are expressions by young people of an inability to cope with the stress that is coming at them. Yet we as adults are remarkably slow to cotton on to what it is our children are needing. The discussion of stress is so low in priority in the school curriculum that it is ordinarily absent. School is one of the generators of stress, but at the same time it is the place where attitudes and habits are learnt that may last for life, at an age when the captive audience is at its most impressionable. It is also a place where the positive use of stress can easily be experienced.

As adults, whether parents, teachers, role-models or friends, how can we best equip our children to deal with the stress they will meet?

★　★　★　★　★

For instance:

There is an excitement to which our children are exposed that motivates them, stimulates them, urges them into experimentation and new experiences, new fascinations.

There is also an excitement that is resorted to as a mask for bewilderment and confusion, anxiety and inadequacy.

If I can prove myself capable of this defiance of authority, then others will admire me and I won't feel so inadequate in other ways.

Do *we* know the difference? Do our children recognize the difference? Can they be helped to do so? Can we *tell* them the difference for them? Do they have to experience the difference for themselves?

With all the current emphasis on parental authority, parental choice, parental control, it seems parents are being encouraged to take their children's compliance for granted. What about the child's own choice? preference? opinion? control? Are we building in them a sense of involvment, of decision-sharing?

★　★　★　★　★

It is salutary to ask questions like these of ourselves. Before offering some ways of answering them, it would be good to look a little closer at the actual present-day experience of childhood.

In the last couple of decades the emphasis has been on stimulation. From the mobiles jiggling in front of the babies' eyes above their cots and on their prams, through the excitability that is kept up on children's telly, to the high expectation of amusement to be provided in the holdidays, our young are in a constant state of hyper-arousal. We spoon-feed them with stimulation to such an extent that they come to depend on it, and quickly complain of boredom if it is allowed to lapse. Novelty, change, challenge, thrills are succeeded by necessarily greater thrills, noise, lights, sensations. We all experience the speed of life today, but we are not all so impressionable.

Stimulation, distraction, diversion are the names of behaviours today; whatever happens we must stop ourselves from pausing and listening. Least of all do we encourage our children to stop and pause.

> It's like being swept along in the race of a tumbling river. When I do want to pause I feel powerless; I can't compete. So I try making a little eddy of my own – it might get me a bit of attention but it might also suck me under.

The tension can grow to such proportions that to explode in aggression is a relief.

Then the explosion has to be re-enacted in order to keep up the level of release. There are many ways in which to do this, all of them guaranteed to aggravate adults. A tense child gets release by:

- ☐ defying authority, whether at home, at school, or in social behaviour;
- ☐ taunting 'fate', playing 'chicken', proving my invulnerability;
- ☐ testing my domination over myself and proving my endurance;
- ☐ exercising power over the vulnerable – bullying, mugging;
- ☐ enjoying the suspense of whether I'll be found out;
- ☐ stimulating excitement to mask depression:
  'I'm scared, but the thing is I like it, I want more'.

Perhaps a large measure of the cause lies in a commonly expressed statement:

> 'Nobody listens! We're told and shouted at and demanded of and told and preached at and told again – *but never listened to.'*

★　★　★　★　★

There's space for a quick anecdote here, to lighten the negatives and highlight the positives.

A granny took her 2½-year-old grandson along the burn for a walk. Just by a patch of shallow rapids they squatted down to watch. 'Can you hear the water sing?' she asked. 'Can you see the water dance?' No more was said, but the little boy remained rapt, motionless and silent, for two long minutes. Then they walked on and talked about other things.

Several days later the little boy returned from a walk with with his father along a different part of the stream. 'Did you hear the water sing?. . . Did you see the water dance?' asked the granny, not really expecting a 'sensible' answer. The boy looked puzzled. 'Water no sing,' he replied, 'Water no play games.'

And then 'adults' think little eyes and ears can't absorb!

STRESS-SKILLS FOR EQUIPPING OUR CHILDREN

☐ *From infancy, reinforce wonder.* Do we take time to let our toddlers listen, wordlessly, to the sounds of water, birds, wind, animals? To look, wordlessly, at insects, spiders' webs, frost, leaves? Letting *them* take in their own impressions, not relaying ours?

☐ *Encourage the practice of stillness* – mulling over the events of the day, reflecting to *themselves* on their experiences of the day, 'gossiping' mentally to *themselves*.

☐ *Listening.* Taking their opinions seriously as they grow older. Asking for, and listening to, their advice. It doesn't have to be acted upon, but it does have to be listened to and taken into account.

☐ *Sharing responsibility* as well as complaints! Developing a mutual dependence in seeing that the chores of the house are done;
sharing decisions about the family menu;
sharing decisions about who to invite for high days;
sharing decisions about colours for re-decoration;
sharing decisions about holidays, schools, how to tackle

difficult family relationship, times of bed, outings, neighbours, etc. . . . *Its called developing mutuality*.

☐ *Trusting* – in the first place, that they won't hurt you,
willingly; and secondly, that there will be occasions when
they could even be right!

☐ *Apologize* when appropriate. Apologize to each other, and
say 'sorry' to another adult in their presence when it
seems right and natural. Accept their apology, or a well-
meant substitute, as necessary.

☐ *Offering a choice*. It is good negotiating tactics whenever
something *has* to be done to make a choice out of it.
'Please do the washing-up' turns into 'Would you rather
finish your programme now and do the washing-up later,
or do the washing-up now while I iron your shirt?'
Learning give-and-take starts early, even before school,
but it has to be kept clear of bargaining and rewarding.

☐ *Help with making decisions*, and staying with them.
Discussing the pros and cons of various possibilities,
without giving the impression that the outcome is a
forgone conclusion, can help the young person see the
situation from all points of view. Then, when the decision
has been made, he/she may want suggestions about how
to resist pressure from their peer group if they are likely
to take a different stand.

Practising how and when to say 'No' can be helpful,
as well as how and when to say 'Yes'.

☐ *Rewarding the trying* as much as the achieving. It is enormously important to establish as early as possible, that
how 'un-success' is dealt with is as significant as success
itself. Failing is *not* failure; it is part of learning and
growing into wholeness. Disappointments, set-backs,
illnesses, lack of instant popularity are all temporary 'un-
successes' that contribute to our total understanding of
life.

☐ *Discovering a stable and practical moral framework* to base
their daily behaviour on. It is likely at first that a young
child will absorb the moral stand of their parents, but this
won't last long unless they are helped to work out for

themselves its strong and weak points. There is a fine distinction between giving them a standard that is strong enough for them to protest against, and not over-reacting when they do.

★   ★   ★   ★   ★

What form of reward do we teach our children to expect? The easy one of instant gratification? Material gifts – sweets, clothes, money? Or the more sustainable gifts that are harder to come by – the achievement of self-set goals, the recognition of worth, the building of values that won't give way?

Rather than repeatedly undermining their views, belittling their responses, disregarding their contributions and then having to make up with a quick compensation of sweet things, how about

Listening:
  Sharing:
    Respecting their own sense of responsibility?

Many adults reflect, when voicing some pearl of practical wisdom. 'As my mother used to say. . .' We crystalize a considerable degree of experience into these pithy sayings, and introducing them to young children can act as a useful short-cut. Each family makes up its own, but these are a sample of some that have proved useful:

COPING PHRASES

- ☐ It's not fair! – Life IS unfair, just get on with it.
- ☐ Why should it happen to me? – Why *shouldn't* it happen to you?
- ☐ Coping with the good moments, that's easy. Coping with the bad moments, that takes something extra.
- ☐ It's not you I don't trust, it's all those others on the road.
- ☐ Anyone can find a fence (offence); it's the clever ones who can find a gate.
- ☐ Can't always have what you want *now* – it's even better later. Looking forward is as great as having.
- ☐ Life is as much about loss as it is about gain; win or lose it's *how* you get there that matters.
- ☐ Other people are imperfect too.

★ ★ ★ ★ ★

AND PLAY WITH THEM!

★ ★ ★ ★ ★

───CHRISTIAN OUTLOOK───

Jesus Christ found it perfectly natural to be 'disputing' – i.e. discussing, reckoning, considering – with the doctors of learning of his day when he was only twelve. As a child he took adults seriously, and as an adult he took children seriously. 'Forbid them not,' he said; that is, he told his friends not to 'prohibit the children from asking' (literal translation of seventeenth-century 'forbid') and the listening that is consequent upon asking. This is rather more than the normally understood interpretation of 'don't stop them coming to my side'.

He wanted children to ask questions. *He wanted to listen to them. Why don't we?*

20

Too many demands

There are those who have many demands, and there are those who feel they have *too* many demands.

It is a fact of life that anyone who shows competency or willingness will have things demanded of them. In part it is a compliment to them that this is so; when someone is asked to do something, built in to the request is the expectation that that person is capable of doing it. Maybe it will mean learning a few extra skills – such as time-management (looked at previously in chapter 9), ordering priorities, delegating reponsibility – but at heart there is a confidence that the task will be carried out effectively. Similarly, those who accept responsibility also have to accept the implication that they are capable of handling it. Even with unexpected demands it is assumed that any necessary restructure can be coped with.

On the other hand, when we find ourselves feeling we are living with *too* many demands – other than those caused by a temporary crisis – we have to look at our lives and our attitudes with meticulous honesty. This is hard.

- ☐ How much of this 'over' demand comes out of *my choice?*
- ☐ How much of it is because I really am the only one who can do it?
- ☐ How much is because I like to be the only one who can do it,
  and to be seen to be the only one who can do it?
- ☐ How much of what I am doing is what I really want to do?

☐ How much is of real use to other people?
☐ How much helps me to feel I am being useful? and to be seen to be useful?
☐ What tactics can I use to increase my effectiveness?
☐ What tactics can I use to minimize this sense I have of too much stress?

STRESS-SKILLS FOR THOSE WITH TOO MANY DEMANDS

Many of these skills overlap management skills, and they are particularly important in lives today as we learn to put up with all the extra pressures outlined in Part One. They include:

1. knowing my own strengths *and weaknesses;*
2. knowing my own sources of 'in-filling' and reward;
3. owning expectations of myself that are realistic;
4. recognizing my own need to demonstrate how over-worked or put-upon or virtuous or superhuman I am;
5. building in time to allow for 'lows', and also time for personal restoration;
6. learning and practising new ways of sorting out what I have to do and when and how to do it;
7. developing relationships that will support what I am trying to do, and be a resource when I need help;
8. collecting coping phrases.

Self awareness
1, 2, 3 and **4** are all part of *self awareness;* this has already been looked at from various angles. It grows by sensing the responses of others to me, weighing up their feed-back, and paying attention to what makes me feel basically confirmed or dis-spirited.

Accepting unlooked-for responsibilities is often the result of 'I feel I ought . . .' This in itself can be a matter of self-affirmation, or it may take the form of 'poor little me, just look at what has been landed upon me'. This is a difficult statement. Sorting it out is crucial to:

the way I feel the stress (being 'put upon', is an exact image of being stressed);
the reactions of others to me; and
the effect I have on those around me.

Trying to see things as being, at least in part, the result of my *choice* makes them immediately easier to bear, and in addition makes it easier for others to bear me.

> Once I realize that wherever I could have said 'No' I have in fact exercised my own choice, I need no longer waste energy on complaining about it. The act of agreeing to do something – doing my neighbour's shopping, organizing an event, caring for a dependant, fund-raising for charity – also implies my willingness to develop the skills to deal with it, and my readiness to call on the contribution of others where it is necessary.

Taking charge of my reponses to the demands made upon me, means that I have to have a clear idea of my own points of hurt and of limitation, those where I am more confident, and of the wells I can turn to for refilling. These may be in people, in nature, in socializing, in the arts, or in my relationship with God. The more demands there are, the more sure I must be of where I can be recharged.

Pacing myself

Stress-skill **5**, building in time, means *pacing myself.* We each have individual rhythms to our lives. More than that, we work to a counter-point of different rhythms coming at us from outside – the pace of our lifestyle, our work, the culture within which we live, the tempo of the different members of those close to us – and of those rhythms that are deep inside. These are the ones that we are often less willing to recognize. Each of us has their own individual biological 'clock' which determines whether we are at our best early in the morning, or in the middle of the day, or later at night. This is the *daily* rhythm. There is also the *weekly* rhythm – whether we use the weekend to recover ourselves or whether it is midweek that is the more routine and less exhausting part. The *monthly* rhythm has considerable significance, particularly for women, though pre-menstrual tension is very variable in its effects on different people. The *annual* rhythm imposes itself on us all, and some people function well in the cold while others are at their best in the heat. Wherever we fit, whatever our preferences, however our personal levels of energy vary, *we must recognize where we are at our best* and, conversely, *where we have to allow for a slowing-down.*

> Whatever the rhythm I discover, it is important that I build it into my plans. When I know I am likely to be 'low', it is foolish to undertake a major new project. When I know a particular event is likely to drain me, it is sensible to build in a time immediately following it to recharge my batteries. The more I want to fit into my life, the more important it is to take into account the basic rhythms on which it is built.

The times for 'in-filling' also vary: they range from those few moments between seeing people, which are used to gather together what has just passed before moving on to the next encounter, to the day off taken after a major weekend conference, or to the five minutes spent lying on my back with my legs raised (on a chair or 'up the wall'?) to rest.

This last may be unorthodox but is extraordinarily revitalizing in a busy day. The basic position can be taken on the floor or on the bed. Raising the legs well up means that:

- ☐ pressure in the circulation is eased, and so the valves of the blood vessels are rested;
- ☐ muscle function is reversed and rested;
- ☐ the natural lumbar curve of the spine, which normally carries so much weight, is temporarily relieved;
- ☐ there is an increase of blood to the brain, carried by gravity;

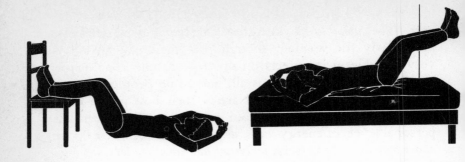

☐ activity is suspended, and mind and emotions can be stilled.

(Note. *It is important that those with high blood pressure do not undertake this*. If there is any increase in discomfort or pain or headache, *do not continue the practice*.)

Programming-in a time for recharging is taken seriously by one of our high-voltage businessmen. Let's call him John:

John jets around the world transporting machines and spare parts to the major motorbike Grand Prix races of the world. When he or his equipment is wanted, it is wanted *now*. The rate, speed, pressure, efficiency and finance of the trips is tremendous. On returning from Florida after one such emergency excursion John had to fly through a hurricane and arrived eventually at Heathrow at 5.30 a.m. His immediate priority (having assured his colleagues by phone that he was safe) was to drive directly to a filled-in quarry on his way home, where he spent three hours bird-watching. Then he was ready to take on the demands of another day.

That is positive stress-control.
John enjoys the pressure, he looks out for it, and lives by it, but equally he takes steps to build-in a return to the 'norm', to the level of being 'at ease'. This practice means he avoids the harmful effects of stress and strengthens his powers of coping.

Pacing myself also includes the skills of saying 'No,' without either giving offence or feeling guilty (objectivity and the proper use of assertion with an unloaded explanation come into this), and the development of time-management skills. These aspects have been discussed previously. Taking time to plan, to build-in spaces for restoration, and to allow for 'highs' and 'lows' of personal output and emotional energy, will help to counterbalance the stress of feeling I have too many demands upon me.

Sorting out what has to be done

Stress-skill **6** means *making lists, ranking priorities*, and *setting goals* – all of which involves taking charge of my own choices and decisions.

Making a list seems at first sight a very elementary thing to do, but it has a great variety of hidden values:

- ☐ I will probably sit down in order to do it.
- ☐ It means the whole day is looked at as an entity, rather than in bits.
- ☐ Each demand or chore is recorded, put outside one's mind, so there is no need for the 'I can't possibly hold it all in' type of feeling.
- ☐ The day can be ordered, given direction, which gets rid of the 'Where on earth do I go next?' type of disorder.
- ☐ All the different tasks can be ranked, and put in a hierarchy of urgency; some will come under a heading of 'must be done today', others will be included under 'would be nice to get done today', and yet a third group would be 'could be put off until tomorrow'.
- ☐ Each item can be crossed off as it is completed – this brings a great feeling of relief, especially if the first job is 'make a list' and it can be deleted straight away. Make sure to include times for meals, space for in-filling pauses, and extra time for jobs done in the slow part of the day.
- ☐ A certain number of minutes can be allocated to each item, so then I can be confident it will all be fitted in. This also enables me to say to an unexpected caller, 'I've just got fifteen minutes. Will that be enough or shall we

make it another time?' That gives them some choice, and they won't feel so put out.

And all this is on a piece of paper, which is itself a 'visual aid' and is outside myself and therefore not subject to my upheavals of anxiety.

Deciding on priorities and setting goals are closely linked. The same job, for instance shopping, may be a high priority on one day – when the larder is bare – and very low on another – when a child falls sick. Goals will also vary from day to day; it is important to learn to break down large and long-term goals into smaller ones that are realistic. If I set myself aims that I can reasonably reach by the end of the day I will know that my time has been constructive; if the aims I set myself are too high I will end the day feeling a failure.

Pacing myself also means recognizing when I need help, where to go for it, who would do the job better than I could anyway, how to ask for it, and how to accept it readily. This all comes into making sure of a –

Support network

Initially my *support network* (stress-skill **7**) will consist of my immediate family and my work colleagues. It will also include my personal reward system. Wider than that are the advisers for the particular area I am feeling stressed about: perhaps this will be the local medical and paramedical or nursing resources; perhaps it will involve careers advisers or design advisers or building advisers; sometimes I will need the advice and counsel of special friends; perhaps I will need the practical help of craftsmen or local specialists in certain areas; there will very likely be times when I need to seek out a particular self-help group or church group – there are a multitude of sources of personal support around. Often it will be up to me to set about finding it. Sometimes I may find it more useful to ask for help anonymously, by post or telephone, while at other times only someone who knows me very closely will do.

If I feel under the stress of having many demands made upon me, it is particularly important to be aware of exactly where I can go for support. And, if possible, to be able to tell them so. This can be made easier if it is seen that a 'benefit' goes to both parties, rather than one being under a sense of obligation to the other.

> It is a matter of using the time-honoured methods of good neighbourliness, of being some mutual help to each other, engaging each other's co-operation, making the most of each person's abilities and gifts, rather than enclosing myself in my own cocoon of the 'I can manage perfectly well on my own, I don't need you' variety.

Coping phrases

It is helpful to collect *coping phrases* (stress-skill **8**). For instance:

- ☐ Maybe I can't *cope*, but by opening up –
  I can *co-operate*.
- ☐ Pottering sometimes is good;
  I must LET-UP to avoid being LAID-UP.
- ☐ Don't fuss at what hasn't got done, just look at what has got done!
- ☐ I said to God – 'It's *so* untidy'; God said to me – 'I don't mind'.

────── CHRISTIAN OUTLOOK ──────

The guilt that is often felt when we don't manage to get it all done is commonly laid at the door of 'Christian' exhortation to be perfect in our duty. But does Jesus Christ himself expect us to feel guilty when we find we are inadequate? Or does he *know* we are inadequate, imperfect, vulnerable, even better than we know it ourselves?

Considering all the emphasis that there has been concerning guilt, this is a staggering fact: in 760 pages of the *Modern Concordance to the New Testament* (DLT 1985) there is NO HEADING FOR GUILT. Under the heading for 'Accuse' there are five sub-headings. Under one of these there are seven references. In only a single one of these is Christ recorded as using the word translated as 'guilty', and this is where he refers to the one unforgivable sin against the Holy Spirit.

Jesus Christ urges us to turn to him for living water, for unconditional love, for mercy and restitution and strength and direction. But he hasn't asked us to laden ourselves with burdens of guilt.

He wants us to acknowledge how often we turn away from him, how much we prefer doing things our way rather than his; but there is no evidence that he wants us to carry around self-manufactured *guilt*. That only makes us less able to cope with life in the way he would have us able to cope.

Perhaps it is only when we realize how inadequate we are, totally inadequate, that we know how totally we depend upon him.

21

Stress in the environment

Environments can be both stressing and stressed. Where the general situation is stressing (that is, where there is over-crowding, poor housing, pollution of the air or earth or water, bad management of resources, unemployment, or abuse of technological developments) the environment itself is stressed. We are now learning how the ecological systems in our environment become disordered and may even disin-tegrate under the stress we put upon them. It has become less and less a matter of 'me against the world', and more and more a matter of me working with the created world to sort out a more mutual partnership. We urgently need a way of working in line with our environment which will restore a balance between us and between people.

All the above conditions of stress in the environment produce anger, frustration and powerlessness. This situation, unchecked, increases disease and dis-order. It becomes imperative to take the situation in hand, to make use of all the energy that has been trapped within it, and put it to work to our advantage instead of against us.

This chapter will take a brief look at the alarms that underlie these various sorts of distress, and then suggest responses that may be useful.

★　★　★　★　★

Chapter 20 concerned the stresses that may be felt by those who have too many demands made upon them. The situ-ation of having too little demand made upon one can produce stress that is just as powerful, but it is of a different order. It often feels like powerlessness.

Powerlessness takes on many guises:

> anger at the insensibility of bureaucracy;
> despair at the distance of intractable landlords;
> ignorance concerning the effects of fertilizers or food additives;
> frustration at being unable to find a job;
> loss of self-esteem and identity at being made 'redundant';
> stress over-load which results from lower levels of spending power, of social enjoyment, of visible productivity, of intimacy (these things can result from being without a paid job for any length of time).

This feeling of powerlessness sets up basic ALARMS:

☐ *Alarm at not being valued.* This feeling of being without significance may lead to irritability, fussiness, loneliness, misunderstandings, just at the point when friendship and support are most needed.

☐ *Alarm at being separated out.* The loss of a job, or status, or money, is too often followed by loss of friends, of identity, of daily routine, of an external framework made up of predetermined goals and structures, just at the point when a strong sense of direction is most needed.

☐ *Alarm at the possible loss of personal choice and control.* The inability to follow one's chosen path brings with it the fear of missing out on preferred goals and rewards. This can come just at the point when these had seemed to be within reach, and the profound disappointment which results means that trust and respect get replaced by suspicion and nervousness. The worst that can happen becomes expected.

All this is on top of the distress of living in a distressed environment. The disadvantage itself may stem from causes that have political, social, or industrial beginnings.

The following poem, written by someone in the queue, puts it well:

We shuffle down toward Box 2
At 10 o'clock.
We are a thrift shop of discarded skills, marked down to
  'present worth':
The trusty hands with thirty years of shaping steel
  available for work at cleaning cars or recycling cotton
  reels.
And his bright hair holding hopes – in his hand
  fresh minted school exams held like a spear
To challenge dragons of industrial might –
But that elusive creature isn't here.
He breathes his fire on afro-asian knights
And me.
Too bad we wish you luck they cried,
But you are far too old and over-qualified.
(Sally Sullivan)

This rather heavy state of affairs has been graphically drawn
by a student. He said that before discussing his difficulties
he felt like a shapeless morass being pulled in all directions:

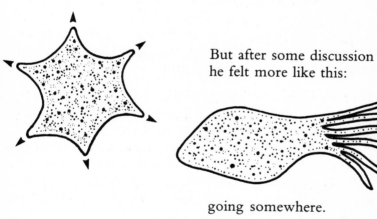

But after some discussion
he felt more like this:

going somewhere.

★　★　★　★　★

The word 'work' derives from the ancient 'wergon', or
Greek 'ergon'; from the identical root comes 'energy'!
  The *Oxford Dictionary* defines 'work' as 'expenditure of
energy' and 'application of effort to some purpose'; so who

is without work? Basically, our self-worth depends on a belief in what we are doing, the way in which we *are* spending our energy, rather than in what we *could* be doing.

STRESS-SKILLS FOR THOSE FEELING POWERLESS

When a group of people whose stress was based on being without paid work was asked, 'What skills are wanted?' they came up with this list:

- ☐ dealing with anger;
- ☐ making relationships better;
- ☐ coping with blame;
- ☐ liking ourselves again;
- ☐ finding direction;
- ☐ rediscovering our worth;
- ☐ information as well as discussion;
- ☐ relaxation techniques.

To these may be added:
- ☐ ways of being creative;
- ☐ affirming areas of own choice and control;
- ☐ encouraging things that move outward, rather than things that feed introspection.

Many of these skills overlap areas that have been looked at before. They can be summarized here as:
- ☐ recognizing the stress and the stressors, as well as the stress-signs;
- ☐ recognizing the energy trapped within the stress;
- ☐ recognizing ways of releasing this energy and channelling it into directions that are *chosen*.

The special emphasis among those living in stressed conditions is to break away from the enervating spiral of 'Poor Little Me'. Yes, the world is unfair. Yes, compassion is rare. Yes, the odds are stacked against me. But there are ways of asserting my own worth in the face of all this.

Am I going to allow the energy of anger, frustration, bitterness, to churn me up, chew me up, change my shape or am I going to use that same energy to work for me in the way I want?

Three basic principles apply:

1. I need someone to whom I can let out the strong emotions within me.

2. I need someone with whom I can share ideas and to whom I can listen.

3. I need someone who needs me as I am now, warts and all.

Probably these needs will best be met *outside* my immediate home.

The whole of this argues for the setting up of a group of like-minded people, who are in similar positions, to work out a direction for *action*.

The chief difficulty of a self-help group is that it may be taken over by some who predominantly want to complain; complaints will be legitimate, but where possible people's imaginations could work on action that is constructive, rather than pulling the situation down still further. Energies can be constructively channeled into looking at such questions as:

- ☐ What can realistically be *done*? Organizing a residents' association? Lobbying an M.P.? Taking on a piece of work ourselves?
- ☐ What is in our own control? Where can we *choose?*
- ☐ What can be adapted – in the environment? in *my* environment? in *me?*
- ☐ Is there someone else, whose needs are different but just as pressing, to whom I can offer my time/skills/ knowledge/care?

Simultaneously, of course, all action that enables me to improve my own personal situation should be taken – looking for a job, applying for better housing, harnessing whatever help is available from the state or the community or the church or industry. The more I *do*, the more results

I achieve, the more my confidence will grow, the more I will be able to persuade others that my 'cause' is worth support.

There are some basic attitudes in these difficult circumstances that need developing:

1. *Determination* not to be put down, nor to be set up, set on one side, pointed out, stigmatized. I know me, and I will not allow myself to be singled out. I shall turn elsewhere to find support that is more worthwhile.

2. *Flexibility* – where one way leads to a dead-end, try another. Sometimes it may be the situation that can be adapted, sometimes it may be me that has to adapt to the situation. Sometimes I may have to dribble for a while; sometimes it may be more effective to confront; at other times I may want to conform, but it will be *my* choice.

3. *Optimism* will not only help me to keep a sense of proportion, it will also mean that other people will relate more easily to me, and that I am more likely to achieve whatever it is I am trying to achieve.

4. *Distancing*, where appropriate, will help me keep from drowning. Learning to switch off sometimes, to remain a little apart, to detach myself from taking everything as if it were personal to me and was my personal responsibility. It will allow others to take their share and keep me in the action a bit longer.

5. *Commitment to change* – and not being too put out when it actually affects me in ways I hadn't expected. The more I accept that change is a *process* and seldom an instant improvement, the more I shall be able to take advantage of the small changes as they occur, however surprising they turn out to be. Trying out those doors that open, instead of getting upset over doors that don't.

Coping hints
Build a structure that includes all of the following points on the grounds that 'if you don't know where you're going you'll probably end up somewhere else':

☐ Construct a time-framework to the day, *and stick to it.*
☐ See someone every day.
☐ Enjoy something every day, and express what is enjoyable.
☐ Do something outside the home for someone/something every day.
☐ Write down each day whatever has been creative about that day.
☐ Make sure of having a safety-valve; don't neglect it, use it.
☐ Plan something achievable every day, and achieve it.
☐ Use imagination to feed hope and keep it alive.
☐ Find out something every day.

────── CHRISTIAN OUTLOOK ──────

In his life-time, Jesus Christ was always the champion of the disadvantaged. Throughout his teaching he urges us to widen our compassion and understanding. He also preached the opportunities that are to be found *within* the situation of being in need. He even called that state 'blessed' because of the extent of the hope and development and release that is opened up when we perceive our own need. *But,* Jesus also knows we can opt out of these challenges by transferring the responsibility on to something or someone else; he is aware of our ability to scape-goat one another. We are only too adept at deceiving ourselves; I have a capactiy for self-delusion which lets me get around those things I find uncomfortable, which is limitless. And then Jesus calls our bluff.

Remember the story of John the Baptist in the wilderness? He had no home, no paid job, no 'proper' clothes or even 'proper' food. And the people flocked to him; they claimed it was to repent and be baptized. But when John was imprisoned by the powerful king they suddenly didn't want to know. They wouldn't support him when it came to the crunch and their own security might be put in danger.

Jesus called their bluff. He asked them bluntly what they had gone out into the desert to see — was it the beauty of nature and its wild plants? (growing things are almost non-existent to the visible eye in the desert of Palestine for most of the year) or was it to gape at a man in luxurious clothes? (who would be more likely be found in the royal palaces); or had they gone out in order to please Herod? (who at the time was interested in John's teaching). Jesus takes our motives and shakes them and turns them back in the form of questions. Has he got our motives right? Have we?

There are very few things that Jesus is actually recorded as condemning. Exploitation of the poor was one of them, but what made him most angry of all was hypocrisy. Doing the right thing for the wrong reason, or saying, 'Look at me, aren't I good?' We all have to watch out for these things, both when we are in need and when we try to care for others.

Christians, in particular, have to be aware of the values of others whom they may be trying to 'help'. It is good to bear in mind the definition of God offered by the Bishop of Durham:

'God is a Presence, a Power, and a Promise.' No pretence.

22
Transitions

The events that are commonly included under the umbrella of 'transitions' are described in chapter 2. This section could equally well have been entitled 'Letting Go' – it covers skills needed for small partings or major bereavements, in different degrees. However, deep grief is felt to be unlike any other experience. Some feel that no matter how many 'little deaths' have been faced and grown through, nothing can pave the way for sudden and tragic bereavement. Every individual experience of it is different, and no one can do the actual experiencing except the griever, however much others may want to offer relief. Most of us have to deal with little deaths more often. The term 'transition' covers all of these changes, and the skills that can apply to them are useful in different circumstances to different degrees. All transitions are important, and they should all be dealt with perceptively rather than just 'letting them happen', without much inkling of what is going on.

STRESS-SKILLS
FOR THOSE FACING A TRANSITION

☐ Where possible, transitions should be *planned for in advance*. This is obvious in many cases, such as marriage, the birth of a new baby, a time in hospital, a holiday, or a new job. But there are implications even in these instances which are less obvious, and which also apply to accidents, theft, and expected death or loss or separation:

Since I am my only tool, whatever happens I must
  continue to look after myself (chapter 9).
The stress of the situation can be counterbalanced with
  times of diversion and even fun.
Everything will take longer because of its unfamiliarity.
So the count-down must start early, and I must not
  expect myself to cope with everything at the last
  minute, even if this is my usual style.
All the practical techniques will be invaluable: making
  lists, ranking priorities, delegating tasks, managing
  time. (These have been described in some detail in
  other chapters.
Making the most of the positives in the phase that is
  passing; taking special pleasure in what I have while
  I have it: these will help minimize my regrets when it
  has passed.
Making real to myself that *everything does change*.

☐ Part of this anticipation will be *letting in some of the hurt*.
Even when the transition is happy, desired, and forward-
looking, change always includes something of loss:

If I allow myself to feel some fear of the unknown, then
  it won't be such a shock when it comes.
I will have to be patient with myself as well as others,
  while the phase of unfamiliarity passes.
I will have made mistakes; there will have been decisions
  I regret; I will sometimes get it wrong. I am
  imperfect, so how can I expect it to be otherwise?
If I can unpack and deal with hurts and bitterness *now*
  rather than allowing them to collect, they won't be
  carried over to the new life. Unresolved resentment
  can weigh heavily; I should do my best to sort it out
  now while it still hangs loose and before it has had
  chance to harden.

☐ Letting in the hurt and the pleasure will help in *letting-go
of the past* when the change does come about.

I am very good at acquiring new goods, getting into new
relationships, establishing my position. What I am not so
good at is letting these go. I even forget to teach my children
how to let go.

My own digestive system is a marvellous analogy of the

healthy way to cope with what I meet – it absorbs what is positive and nurturing: and discards what is negative and harming.

Clinging is the response of small children, yet as an adult I too try to cling to the things I want. Perhaps growing up emotionally as well as physically means letting go, learning not to lean too hard but to stand up by myself. Some of the collection of battered suitcases I carry around with me that are full of things I no longer use could be put down. I will feel lightened and released when I am able to unshackle myself from them, and find it easier to go forward.

☐ *Adjusting to the compensations.* In many circumstances these can be looked forward to and happily anticipated, as long as not too much is expected at once. Just as letting go will be spasmodic – sometimes it will feel easy and at others the clinging will be worse – so will the pleasure in the compensations be uneven. Sometimes life will be rosy, but at others the 'Was it all worth it?' will be overwhelming.

As long as I hang on to the fact that these ups and downs are part of the stress of change, and will pass, it will be easier to keep steady.

Sometimes I will have to parent myself. There are some things no one can work through except myself. It may be that at times I have to do this on my own, however much I would like another to help me. At least I will have the knowledge of their concern, and, later on, that the task has been done.

Best of all will be the new ideas, new insights, new experiences that will be just around the corner. Expecting them will make it easier for them to arrive.

Gradually the realization will come that life does get balanced out again, that it still goes on going on, and that there is creativity all around to support it. I will survive, I will refashion a new shape. The world does recover.

★　★　★　★　★

Perhaps those who have understood their own transitions are

better at understanding others. Listening has been described before, but for those who are deeply bereaved there are some additional points to bear in mind.

Most grieving people prefer to talk about their lost love, particularly the pleasant times, and looking at pictures with happy memories. Friends sometimes think that this may open up feelings that have been sucessfully covered over and that talking about things that have gone may reactivate the sorrow and distress. It may allow sorrow to be exposed and expressed, but it will also allow the good and strong things to be re-enacted and brought to the front. Most important, it will give a chance to the griever to share what most engrosses them.

Take a close look at these words:

SUCCOUR	SUPPORT	SUSTAIN
from sub-currere	sub-portare	sub-tenare
literally, to run	*to carry from*	*to hold from*
underneath	*underneath*	*underneath*

They all refer to *being there from under*. No mention of 'pulling them up' or 'dragging them along'!

When listening to a friend recovering from a grave loss, I must be prepared to hear things I don't want to hear. Anger, blame, scape-goating, rancour. There is seldom any point in rationalizing with these feelings; they are all valid reactions to hurt. Resisting them won't stop them, but releasing them might lance the wound. If I can just stay alongside my friend, without reinforcing or rejecting the negative explosions, I may be able to provide the steadiness that is being looked for.

Sometimes it is not even the 'Aren't you wonderful, you are coping so bravely,' that is needed, it is permission to be less than wonderful, to share the distress, to allow the griever to stop coping for a moment and let out the bewilderment, that is the more valuable. And then perhaps never to refer to the incident again, if that is best for the griever.

Someone said recently, 'The best fruit grows out of a

pile of muck, but that doesn't mean the muck has to be turned over and over.'

Two further responsibilities belong to the listener:
- ☐ Remember that decisions made within six months of a sudden loss (any grave loss, not only death) can be unreliable. Emotions are too unsteady and may lack long-term value. Although quick solutions may seem highly desirable to all concerned, their resolution may not last.
- ☐ Be ready for those moments when the griever wants to lay aside the grief for awhile and have a bit of irreverent diversion. If the gloom lifts, take advantage of it – make the most of it!

————CHRISTIAN OUTLOOK————

Think about this . . .

The most popular and familiar images that Christ used to apply to himself are about

passage and movement and growth.

> I am THE WAY
> I am THE DOOR
> I am THE WATER
> I am THE VINE

After all, he introduced the greatest transition of all: 'I AM THE RESURRECTION . . .'

Part Four

LIVING AT EASE WITH UNCERTAINTY

So here we are at the conclusion. Much of this book has been about skills and attitudes. What about attributes and beliefs? Most of the pronouns have been *me, my* and *I*; what has happened to *him, her* and *them?*

My family and my neighbour are my basic concern. It is when I have learned to live at ease with stress – by adopting certain skills and attitudes – that they will find me easier to live with. If that leads me to absorb certain attributes and beliefs, it is more likely that life with me will be easier for *him* and *her*.

It's unreal to extract me away from others for long, so the last few pages will be about *us*.

* * * * *

We all spend a great deal of our energy, our time, and our ingenuity in trying to make sure we are safe. Safe from accidents, safe from theft, safe from violence, safe from failure, safe from being found out, safe from poverty and hunger, safe from looking foolish and being in the wrong. Our lives and health and homes and jobs and property are rightly important to us, and we contrive elaborate tactics to reassure ourselves that we are in control of them, those things that are in our particular section of the universe.

At a wider level, we have constructed mammoth government departments to devise structures of law and order and national security, and we spend a gross amount of public money on national defence. Entire professions are built on arranging insurance against risk, and vast resources are put into keeping our bodies, homes, food, schools, cars, hospitals, equipment and all public places 'safe'.

It is a task that has no end because we can never be wholly safe. Uncertainty, risk, and violence are in-built; they are part and parcel of our human make-up.

Many of the games we played as children were about controlling the uncontrollable, and about stress-proofing against risk. Sometimes this desensitizing works; but to remain coolly insensitive indefinitely can restrict the growth of our maturity.

To be truly mature we must regain our vulnerability and hold it together with an acceptance of risk.

★ ★ ★ ★ ★

Without risk, without stress, life would soon lose its taste; it would become innocuous, flat, predictable, with unrelieved boredom. The 'risk' we choose to take adds excitement and zest to life, but we like to feel it is calculated, controlled, and that we are in charge of it. Being prepared to accept the risk we *don't* choose can help us to grow. Challenge and change give us chances of moving on. Taking the stress in hand and putting the energy within it to work creatively for us is what this book has been all about. Gathering skills to handle stress gives us confidence to meet it with good cheer; and at those times when we are feeling woeful and doleful it gives us a bit more trust in moving on.

The sum of these skills is recognize, relate, release, relax, reflect. The sum of the attributes we need could be:

☐ *Flexibility* towards what might happen.

If we plan to give a party in mid-winter we take the risk

that snow might prevent the guests coming; it would
therefore be wise to arrange food that can be stored in
the freezer and have an alternative date just in case plans
have to change.

Being prepared for a variety of ways through a problem,
lessening it's rigidity, makes it more interesting anyway.

□ *Being able to adjust* to what does happen; accommodating,
fitting in.

If our plane is cancelled there is little point in reacting
with foot-stamping and resolutions never to fly again;
we would simply be hurting ourselves by our behaviour,
and we would be the only ones to be hurt. Containing
the impatience and reordering our plans would be a
quicker way to getting what we really want.

Being accommodating is also very infectious – others seem
want to join in the new start too.

□ *Responding to the now;* everything is passing. It is *now* that
is crucial.

The trees in Kew Gardens had been planted, nurtured,
protected, admired, painted for over two hundred years
before they were bowled over in the storms of one night.
Yet there had been two hundred years of *nows* for
people to enjoy. They hadn't *not* been enjoyed in case
they might fall down one day. But even they weren't
permanent.

Not only is *now* more significant, to make it real *now* reduces
regret later.

Maturity is the measure of our ability to adapt.

★　★　★　★　★

Our personalities, our emotions, our physical nature, our
ideas and our environment are in a permanent state of flux;
intimate, constant movement in answer to changing situations. Why do we try so hard to grab at experience and
fossilize it, to encase it in a stable, see-through matrix, like

those ossified sea-horses in perspex cubes? The interest lies in being open and fluid and ready for what is coming.

$$\star \quad \star \quad \star \quad \star \quad \star$$

Perhaps, in order to live at ease with stress and make the most of the movement and flux in our lives we should take as our model the amoeba, or a bean-bag. We met them at the outset; perhaps the association is clearer now. They both adapt their shape to whatever comes without either splitting open or altering their make-up. They accept and adjust without damaging what's inside.

Perhaps, too, we can take to heart the definition of health, or *wholeness*, that was devised by the philosopher Pericles five hundred years before Christ:

'That state of moral, mental and physical well-being, that enables one to face any crisis with the utmost facility and grace.'

'Facility' is ease, and in this context 'grace' is good will. So:

☐ The more we are at ease with our own shape and adapt it to meet whatever comes, the more comfortable we shall be to live with, and the more comfortable we shall find living is.

☐ The more we can accept muddle and disorder and uncertainty without distress, the better we shall handle stress.

☐ The more we can take on board the search rather than the finding, the less disturbed we will be when our solutions don't work.

For all plans can be compromised; all rules can have exceptions; all boundaries can be broken.

It is only our Lord God who created the whole system
Who encompasses the puzzle,
and who makes sense of it.

————CHRISTIAN OUTLOOK————

The Christian would say that the only certainty we have is that we are loved — totally loved, unconditionally loved. EMMANUEL, God is with us; it is we who find it difficult to believe this love is total and unmerited.

We want to feel we deserve love, to earn it. Paradoxically we hang on to a conviction that we have not done well enough, that we are not worthy of love, and that we ought to be punished. A black worthlessness leads us to feeling guilty. What does Christianity say about guilt — after all, it's all part of 'being religious' isn't it?

In the last great discussion at their last great meal on this earth Jesus Christ insisted to his disciples that he had come neither to judge nor to condemn. His last prayer was not one of blame or bitterness at how his mission had been twisted, but one of giving and of longing. He speaks to his Father: 'I loved those you have given me, so I have given them the glory you gave to me, *That they may be one, as we are one*. . . completely one, with me in them and you in me.' No vestige of retribution, or accusation, or dishonour! Christ wants us to feel loved, wanted, belonging, whole.

Christ knew about stress — we have seen that before — and he knows our tendency to feel guilty when we perform less than perfectly. But he also knows we are IMPERFECT. So if we *start* from that knowledge, it won't be so much a matter of us feeling we are falling from a height, so much as starting from a position of total dependence; total abandonment to, and total reliance upon, God's grace and God's love.

When I am totally dependent upon Christ I will not only offer him my joy and confidence, but also my sickness, sadness and sin. Perhaps more important still, I will throw on to him my puzzlements, doubts and confusions. He will accept them all, unconditionally. I know I won't get the whole answer back, but at least there *is* an answer, and I know he knows it. I know I shall see it bit by bit, as I become capable of doing so. None of us will receive the whole answer until after we die.

> Total dependence is on-going. It lasts a lifetime and more. Just as my need is continuous, it is also continuously supplied. I know therefore that however imperfect I am, however inadequate, however continuously needy, I am not *trash*. Repentance gives me an instant solution to guilt – when I repent I shall feel washed, forgiven, my hands will again be clean. But my inadequacy will continue; and because of this I can continue to depend, to become more whole, move more towards becoming one with Christ, ceaselessly, unstoppably, eternally. Maybe it's a difference between wanting to be sanitized, made clean and kept protected, and yearning to be sanctified, made more whole, more holy.

It's rather like dust particles. When specks of dust accumulate on the top of my desk they are dark, flat, useless rubbish and I want to get rid of them. But when the sun streams through my window, and the same dust specks dance in the brilliant sunshine, they are no longer trash, but radiant particles floating and swirling, reflecting the light of the sun. They are dependent, swinging in the air and relying on the sunbeam for light and support.

Another thing that Jesus said at that final get-together was: 'I, the Light, have come into the world so that whoever believes in me need not stay in the dark any more.'

Dame Julian knew all about light, and she is very light-hearted. She says we all 'shall be solaced and mirthed' with Christ, and that 'our soul shall never rest till it cometh to Him, knowing that He is fullness of joy, homely and courteous, blissful and very life'.

Living *is* being involved with paradox, turmoil, having no complete answers, no complete safety. There is no other responsible way but to be dependent. But the more we depend upon God, the more we find we can affirm the Love, Faith and Hope that are his.

If there were no risk, we would have no grounds
   for *hope*;
   If there were no uncertainty, we would have no
      grounds for *faith:* and
      If there were no darkness, we would have no
         grounds for *love*.

★   ★   ★   ★   ★

He said not, 'Thou shalt not be tempested, rather
He said, 'Thou shalt not be overcome'.
(Dame Julian)

★   ★   ★   ★   ★

A lot of the time we may be preoccupied with the knots in
our lives. Sometimes we can see nothing but knots. Different
coloured knots, different sized knots, but nonetheless knots.
Then it seems true that we are the carpet workers, on the
under side of a vast Persian carpet, working away at our
own small part of the whole, because we are unable to
perceive it all.

Nor can we see the other side, where the Creator and
Designer of the carpet oversees the finished effect.

It is he alone who can make sense of the whole.

It is he alone who delivers us from non-acceptance,
   from not being good enough.

It is because he invites our dependence that we can live
   in uncertainty.

Finally, since this book was conceived in prayer and has been
unfolded in prayer, the last words should be those of prayer:
   Lord, may it be an instrument of your peace; but it is yours,
   to do with according to your will. Amen

RECOMMENDED READING
AND ACKNOWLEDGEMENTS

The list of books and authors that bear upon Wholeness is vast: almost everything we read influences the approach of wholeness or its distancing. Ideas which bring wholeness nearer may come from novels or poetry, professional literature, social philosophy or holy writ, but most of all they grow from contact with people. So the following is a list of *people* who have particularly influenced me; most of them have published, and any books by any of them are to be highly recommended for further reading.

Elizabeth M. Anderson
Michael Argyle
Eric Berne
Anthony Bloom
Meg Bond
Audrey Livingston
   Booth
Maria Boulding
Christopher Bryant
George Campbell
Mother Mary Clare
J.M. Déchanet
Helene Dicken
Eric Erikson
Erving Goffman
Michael Gresford-Jones
Jean Grigor
John Hare

Thomas Harris
Giles Harris-Evans
Paul Hauck
David Hay
Barrie Hopson and
   Mike Scally
Gerard Hughes
Dame Julian of
   Norwich
Martin Kelsey
Amber Lloyd
Jane Madders
John Main
Anthony de Mello
Thomas Merton
Laura Mitchell
Patrick Pietroni
Sonia Ponter

Robert Reid
Carl Rogers
Cicely Saunders
Robert Sharpe
Ann Shearer
Herbert Slade
Michael Stancliffe
Ian Sutherland
John V. Taylor
Paul Tournier
Esther de Waal
Neville Ward
Jean Wardell
John White
Rosemary White
Jim Wilson
Michael Wilson
Sula Wolff

And, of course, each member of the various groups with whom, over the last 30 years, I have shared the approach to wholeness in mind, body, soma, and spirit; each one of them has coloured my experience and thinking.

☐ Without the unswerving boosts to my swerving confidence given me by Lesley Riddle, the DLT editorial director, this book would not have seen daylight.

☐ Last but by no means least, my thanks are due to my marvellous family, to my husband and our four daughters for their patient ears – and appetites! – while this book has been in the making.

INDEX

Words that appear most commonly in this book are not listed here. These words include 'behaviour', 'friend', 'stress' and 'work'. They speak for themselves on nearly every page of the text. Page references to main entries are in bold.